In Ho...  ...

Aurelius D. Khan

and

Mona Moors Tasker

Both of whom longed to see

the day when the record

would at last be set straight

and a great man properly celebrated.

Finally, it is done!

Hallelujah!

# George P. Tasker: A Man Ahead of His Times
By Douglas E. Welch

Copyright 2001
ISBN: 0-9646682-1-1

For additional available titles, consult the Anderson University website at www.anderson.edu/aupress. Inventory and sales are through Warner Press, Anderson, IN. To order this or other Anderson University Press books:

    Phone:  1-800-741-7721
    Fax:     1-800-347-6411
    Email:   wporders@warnerpress.org

Cover design by Kerry Shaw.
Published with the assistance of the Church of God
   (Anderson) Historical Society, Dr. Merle Strege, President,
   and the Ministerial Education Program of Anderson
   University, Dr. Fred Shively, Director.
Printed by Evangel Publishing House, Nappanee, IN, U.S.A.

ANDERSON UNIVERSITY PRESS

# FOREWORD

The Church of God movement that emerged during the 1930s differed markedly from the movement of scarcely twenty years earlier. The decades from 1915 to 1935 stand certainly among the most critical periods in the entire history of the Church of God (Anderson); quite arguably they are the most important. The fully institutionalized church fellowship that emerged from this period scarcely resembled the loose association of congregations that had entered it. A dominant feature of these years of change is the process of institutionalization.

In 1915, only two organized entities conducted business and oversight responsibilities for the Church of God (Anderson). The older of these was the Gospel Trumpet Company, soon to be headed by F.G. Smith. In his mid-thirties, Smith had risen rapidly to the position of Editor of the *Gospel Trumpet*, the organ of the Church of God. The *Trumpet* was, quite literally, older than the Church of God movement itself. For *de facto* reasons, if none other, the movement looked to the Gospel Trumpet Company and the Editor for organizational leaders as well as its doctrinal voice.

The only other organizational entity to stand alongside the formidable authority of the Gospel Trumpet Company and its Editor was the Home and Foreign Missionary Board, organized in 1909. The Missionary Board initially referred to itself as the Missionary Committee. When one asks, "Of what larger organization was it a committee?" the only possible answer in those years was "the Gospel Trumpet Company."

In 1917, the Church of God began living through a remarkable departure from the structural simplicity of its first almost fifty years. The Gospel Trumpet Company abandoned its original communal organization, emptied its "Home" of all employees and began paying cash salaries and wages. The fledgling Anderson Bible Training School moved into the vacant building. The next decade witnessed the creation of the Board of Religious Education and Sunday Schools, the re-organization of the missionary work into separate boards for home and foreign missions, the Spanish Evangelistic Association, and the General Ministerial Assembly under which all these new boards functioned–the Gospel Trumpet Company included. In that same decade, the movement also divided along racial lines, creating the National Association of the Church of God.

Within a generation, a movement that had come into being protesting the human organization of the Bride of Christ seemed to have repeated the same mistake. At the beginning of the period, the people of the Church of God believed that the Holy Spirit, who gifted men and women for positions of service thereby distributed power through the church. Before the period of institutionalization concluded, power appeared to be distributed through and according to a bureaucratic hierarchy controlled by a very small circle of ministers.

Rapid organizational change rarely occurs without cost. Sometimes that cost can be very high and, tragically, not infrequently paid out in human coin. The story of George Tasker is such a tale. In the opening decades of the twentieth century, Tasker was one of the best and brightest of Church of God ministers and missionaries. He was one of several courageous and talented North Americans who served alongside an equally talented group of Indian converts to Christianity in the early days of the Church of God mission in India. Nevertheless, by the end of 1925 the Missionary Board of the Church of God had dismissed Tasker as a rebellious missionary who threatened to sow seeds of heresy throughout the Indian church.

The word "heresy" suggests another aspect of the changes brewing in the Church of God movement from

1915 to 1935. Even as its polity was changing, so also new voices began to question elements of Church of God doctrine as they had been laid out in Smith's books and editorials. Most of these voices remained muted until the late 1920s and after. Their silence left Tasker virtually alone as the earliest to publicly criticize some of Smith's views, criticism that Smith did not take lightly or well. The doctrinal dispute is interwoven with the movement's changing polity in the story of Tasker's dismissal.

Not only George Tasker, but also many of the people who moved to dismiss him had been caught in the new forms of organization and theological change that combined to alter dramatically the life of the Church of God movement. Like classical tragedy, Douglas Welch's story leaves us with the impression that the leading characters in this tale could scarcely have acted in a manner other than the one they chose. Also in the tragic manner, many of these people lived to express regret for many of those actions.

Professor Welch tells us this story in a familiar tone. He is familiar with his subject well beyond the scope of academic biography. The elderly Tasker was his friend and mentor. Welch *knows* his subject. Readers need to be aware of the particular biases of writers who undertake to write the biographies of their friends. Welch so warns us himself and produces an evenhanded account of the people on both sides of the issues that separated Tasker from the Church of God leadership.

Professor Welch also tells a story that is clearly familiar with the sources that bear on it and familiar with the Church of God movement that is this story's context. Lastly, he tells this story in a familiar voice. To read this book is to enter into an informal conversation with an informed and wise friend who is utterly uninterested in striking a pose. Welch simply wants us to understand.

I often tell my students, undergraduate and graduate alike, that the study of history is the study of us. There are those who study the past simply out of an antiquarian motivation; they are curious to know what life was like in some other place and time. Professor Welch writes out of a very different motive. He writes to inform us about a man whose life and conflicts contributed to the making of the Church of God (Anderson) of which present day readers may be a part.

As Welch tells it, Tasker's story is thus in some measure our story. When we learn that story more completely we may improve not only our self-understanding, but also our vision of what it is that we are called to do.

> — Merle D. Strege
> Anderson University
> Church of God Historian

# TABLE OF CONTENTS

John A.D. Khan

Floyd W. Heinly and Mosir Moses

J.J.M. Nichols Roy

Josephine McCrie

Mona Moors

Above photo courtesy of Irene Engst
and Gerdie Millier

Moundsville VA, 1905. George P. Tasker, second from left. (To his left is E.E. Byrum )

George and Minnie Tasker (c. 1912)

The Taskers, Lahore, India (c. 1915)

# INTRODUCTION

I almost wrote this book in 1979. The centennial celebration of the Church of God was on the horizon and friends were urging me to produce a biography of George Pease Tasker, who had been my mentor and inspiration–a kind of centennial salute to a great man in the early years of the Church of God, a man who had been either largely written out of the histories of the "movement," or about whom so little was known that not much could confidently be said. (And historians do like to say things confidently. Whether or not they should is much debated among them, at least the more insightful among them.)

But I'm glad now I bided my time. In 1979–so I have come to realize–I didn't know enough generally to write a book about anything. I was at the beginning of an academic career that forced me, because of my varied teaching assignments, to buckle down and learn as much as I could in a wide variety of fields of study. Those teaching assignments consumed most of my time, making major research and writing all but impossible. Now, even after 22 years, I'm just getting a good start at learning some of the things I need to know. And I'm certainly a great deal less consumed now that I've retired from teaching.

So, I'm ready now to take up the task I laid aside in 1979. Well, not really aside. Collecting material relating to Brother Tasker's [1] life and ministry has been a long and continuous quest. I've written many letters. I've interviewed

---

[1] Throughout this book, I will use "Brother" in referring to Tasker. That is how I knew him and all I ever heard him called, except by his wife and his colleague, John D. Crose. In my growing up days in the Church of God in Western Canada, "Brother" and "Sister" were commonly used by almost everyone. I find it a comfortable practice.

people, sometimes traveling a lot of miles to do so. I've browsed for many, many hours in early *Gospel Trumpets* and *Missionary Heralds.* I've read all of the relevant Missionary Board correspondence, Minutes, Reports, and other related archival material—of which we now have a great deal in Church of God Archives. I even made an extended trip to India to the places where the Taskers lived and worked and interviewed people who had known the Taskers well.

Over these past twenty years, I've managed to collect a fair amount of archival material which—apart from the thick file of research material in my possession—is now held in the Archives. Very little of that was available in 1979. It may be, I think, that we now have collected nearly all of the relevant material still in existence. Many of the persons to whom I am most indebted for their contribution are now deceased: A.D. Khan; John D. Crose; R.R. Byrum; H.C. Heffren; and Mona Moors Tasker. So I'm glad I didn't lay the collecting aside along with the writing and publishing.

In these years of collection I have been disappointed on occasion to find that archival materials have simply vanished. You've heard it before. "Oh, we didn't know that stuff was of any value to anyone. We threw it out long ago." But at no point was I even half so downhearted as when H.C. Heffren, a long-time and faithful friend of Brother Tasker, wrote to me telling me that a box of Tasker papers given to him by Brother Tasker's widow, Mona Moors Tasker, had been inadvertently thrown out by someone cleaning up old *Gospel Contact* papers and files thought no longer to be needed.

While I quite understood how that could have happened, I was almost sick with disappointment. Mona Moors Tasker had told me that the box contained some personal diaries and other papers relating to Brother Tasker's years with the Church of God before the "painful separation." I had waited anxiously to find out if they were still available and was deeply distressed to learn of their loss. But those things happen.

In fairness, I must add that Brother Heffren was no less distressed than was I. No viable Archives existed in the Church of God in those days, so the office of the *Gospel*

*Contact* in Camrose, Alberta, was as good a bet as any. Just another instance of "might have been." This one was just a lot more personal. Thinking of it even now, I feel impoverished. But on with the task at hand.

## A Man and His Influence

During my life in the Church of God over the past 50 years, I have been deeply influenced by key persons who have mentored, befriended, and supported me–in spite of my life-long tendency to stubborn independence of thought. I think of my first pastor, William P.C. Rabel, who was a good friend and a much needed stabilizing influence in the life of an 18-year old convert from the Jehovah's Witness tradition. Others, including H.C. Gardner, H.C. Heffren, Gordon Schieck, Will Ewert, Milo Chapman, Wilma Perry, and Lester Crose, all helped make it possible for me to remain vitally linked with the Church of God.

But none has played such a formative role in my life and career as has George Pease Tasker. It was my good fortune to sit at his feet, quite literally–on a fine rug woven somewhere in India, I think it was–and to be taught by him. It was there that I began to develop a commitment to the missionary cause of the church and, without knowing it at the time, to good scholarship and scholarly study and exposition of the Scriptures. It was there I learned to love good books and to respect intellectual rigor and honesty.

It is with deep nostalgia and gratitude that I recall the many hours he spent in expounding the Scriptures to me, in explaining important theological issues, in reminiscing about his missionary experiences in India and the Near East, and in prayer and devotion. At the time, the effects of this were incalculable–and perhaps are even to this day.

I spent many evenings and most rainy days–when it was too wet to work in the orchards–at the Taskers' penthouse apartment at 333 Eckhard Avenue in Penticton, British Columbia. How well I recall their warm and gracious hospitality, the simple meals shared together, the hot chocolate and evening devotions, and the fleeting hours spent in the study of the Scriptures and in discussion of missionary work and India. They had very little, but what they had they shared with glad and willing hearts. I was probably a pest, but the warmth and hospitality they so graciously extended to a 19-year old seemed endless.

Our relationship was warm and close. Brother Tasker's usual form of address to me was a very grandfatherly, "My boy." His widow once told me, "My husband had a very special affection for you and Richard Yamabe.[2] He thought of you as his sons in the faith." As a young pastor, fresh out of Bible college, I suppose I unconsciously patterned  my own preaching and teaching after his–content, of course, not style.

In 1956, he and his third wife, Mona Moors Tasker, came to Chilliwack, British Columbia, where I was pastor, to lead us in a Missions Emphasis week. He was delighted when I told him of the experience of my own call to missionary service, but expressed keen disappointment that God had not seen fit to call me to India. Africa was undoubtedly a great and needy field, he assured me, but not nearly so great and needy as India. But, then, he lived and breathed India; it was in his blood and bones. No place on earth could compare with it–and he was a widely traveled man!

## A Necessarily Subjective and Biased View

So I am not,  by any measure, either unbiased or objective–two words I hear with alarming frequency among historiographers–alarming because such words all to often serve as a quasi-scientific mask for as much bias and subjectivity as can be found anywhere. They function, not to convince me of the possibility of being either, but only to arouse my suspicion. All too frequently they constitute a claim to final and unquestionable authority–which may or may not be grounded in any discernible fact.

One of my anthropological "gurus" is Clifford Geertz,

---

[2] Long-time professor and Dean at Alberta Bible Institute (now Gardner College), then for many more years editor and publisher of the *Gospel Contact* and special assignment missionary to Kenya and Japan. Incidentally, perhaps, also my brother-in-law.

now associated with Princeton University. In his most recent book, *Available Light: Anthropological Reflections on Philosophical Topics* (2000), he talks about the limits of all human knowledge. We must recognize the fact, he says, that we are "positioned (or situated) observers" (or participants) seeing from within the events we seek to describe and understand. We cannot, then, stand somewhere above events as detached and unbiased observers. These "views from nowhere," he concludes, can of course be constructed and can be "immensely useful." *"But thus constructed, they are in fact, a particular variety of view from somewhere. . ."* (p. 137, italics mine).

Mine, then, is not a view from "nowhere," for the simple reason that no such place exists. "Disincarnate knowing," as Geertz terms it, is humanly impossible. All of us are, in one way or another, biased, biased in ways that our personal and community situatedness may prevent us from recognizing. But that is not our biggest problem. Being honest about our situatedness and its effects on our viewing is usually where we'll have the most trouble.

So I'm not troubled by any misplaced accusations of bias. In my lexicon, bias is simply an angle of vision: I see things from my point of view. And subjectivity is a necessary human condition: it is I who see, not someone outside of me pretending not to be I. So it is I who present this view of George Pease Tasker. It is a view; and it is I whose view it is (and for that reason I tend to write in the first person–often viewed as a no-no in the scholarly world in which this supposedly objective and unbiased writing is demanded). Other views certainly are possible, therefore, but all views are *not* equally good or equally appropriate to the data. "That's one opinion," does not apply here.

I labor under no illusion that my view is authoritative or definitive. But it is, I think, a carefully informed view. And, I hope it is fair and honest–as much as I can make it so. I'm well aware that primary historical documents can all too easily be misread. So I've done all within my power to read the documents carefully and honestly–while holding my own prior views on the subjects in question as loosely as possible. In my view, such intellectual honesty is a necessary part of being a genuinely moral person–without which spirituality is a mere illusion. Brother Tasker would, I'm sure, expect such honesty. He was that kind of person.

I revere the memory of George Pease Tasker. But I am a research scholar, not a hagiographer. I have no desire to make him out a supersaint, someone larger than life, more sanctified and committed to Christ than all others. My own work on the life of David Livingstone of Africa turned me away from that kind of biography. Livingstone was a deeply committed servant of Christ, but was, nonetheless, a surprisingly humanly flawed man. In the hands of his many biographers, however, he had become larger than life, standing above all human frailties and failures.

Brother Tasker was certainly a man of his times—and a man of very real human frailties. All the same, he was thought by most who knew him—though obviously not all— to be a deeply spiritual and Christ-centered man. He was as human as the rest of us. And, like the rest of us, it was his humanity that so frequently got in his way and came between him and others—something which pained him to tears at times. Friends were very dear to him and it distressed him deeply when misunderstandings and rifts occurred for one reason or another.

He longed for the healing of the rift between him and the Missionary Board of the Church of God that caused the painful separation in 1924. For many years, it was an abiding grief, never far from his mind. Eventually, he was able to effect reconciliation with some of the Missionary Board members and the Board itself a dozen years later admitted to him that it had been hasty and unwise and expressed its deep regret to him. More on that subject later. But, had Brother Tasker been more patient in the first place, more conciliatory, less sharp in his criticisms, less outspoken, the dismissal by the Missionary Board and his virtual excommunication from the Church of God (Anderson, Indiana) might have been avoided.

*Might*, I say. Personally, at this point, after reading all the correspondence and Minutes available concerning this case, I'm not even half persuaded. It may be that Brother Tasker's vision was simply too large for the Church of God at that point in its structural and theological evolution. Today, most of us would agree with him—many perhaps even more than I. I've always been unusually resistant to intellectual cloning. Thinking for myself and avoiding group think have been two of the passions of my life. By the time I had graduated from Bible college in 1954, I occasionally disagreed even with Brother Tasker—and stood my ground.

But his vision in the teens and twenties of the twentieth century was too radical, too threatening for those who were so sure of their own vision. As I heard personally from both John D. Crose, Tasker's younger friend, colleague, and supporter, and A.D. Khan, eldest son of John A.D. Khan: "Brother Tasker was too impatient. He got too far ahead and needed to wait for the Church to catch up. He was a man ahead of his times." And thus the title of this book.

I then offer this highly subjective portrayal—but, I hope, a rigorously researched and reasoned portrayal—on a broad canvas, not because it provides me greater opportunity to grind a personal axe or two and because I have discovered that the data from which histories are constructed can be so manipulated that mice become elephants—or the other way around. Not at all! I consider the apologetic use of history to "prove" what one has already concluded on other grounds to be true as a regrettable misuse of history. Further, I don't believe history "proves" anything, *historians* do. Human events do not come with ready-made interpretive voices.

### Setting the Record Straight

What is it I'm trying to do, then, by writing such a biography at this time if I'm not planning to use such interesting data as a political or ideological platform? My primary concern is simply *to set the record straight.* Brother Tasker was an integral and important part of the Church of God, spanning at least the second generation of its history. But he has been largely ignored in the early writing of our history. It is as if he had been an insignificant person off on the fringe of things—which he most surely was not.

Charles Ewing Brown, in *When the Trumpet Sounded* (1951), had the most to say about him, devoting about a page to a description of him in the early years, but dismissing everything thereafter with the sentence: "And so on for a long and interesting life spent mostly in missionary work in India" (p. 203). It's the "and so on" that concerns me. And it is that "and so on" which is important to us historically. But Brother Tasker was incidental to the story Brother Brown was trying to tell. Writing about him would have diverted him from his apologetic task.

Brother Tasker should not have been incidental to Thaddeus Neff (*Our Missionaries*, 1956, pp. 30-31), however. After all, he wrote an "Introductory" for Brother Neff's book. Here his entire missionary life after 1924, a span of 23 years, is summed up in the sentence, "Later years were spent in Calcutta, and in Bangalore, South India" (p. 31). As with Brother Brown, a virtual curtain of silence is drawn across the stage of history.

But, so it turns out, it is an embarrassed silence. Brother Tasker eschewed the cardinal "come-out" doctrine of the Church and opposed it in both action and writing. He quarreled vigorously with the Missionary Board over its India policies and was "fired." He then appealed to a group of former Church of God pastors–many of whom had also rejected "comeoutism"–and their former Church of God congregations for support to enable him to continue his missionary work in India. "A long and interesting missionary life in India" was probably as far as anyone wanted to go with that story. Not too inspiring or uplifting.

But that is only part of the story–and not even the most significant part for us. The rest of the story, seen in its full context, changes everything. If a "villain" is to be found in the real story–and that may be doubted–it is not Brother Tasker. The way he handled the conflict with the "influential brethren" of the Church and the Missionary Board (who were not fully identical, but considerably so)– at least in the beginning–served only to make things worse. But, in spite of that, he was the sinned against, rather than the sinner he was made out to be.

In the long run, so it turns out, that really didn't matter anyway. Not only was Brother Tasker a man ahead of his times, he may have been too far ahead. The gap had become too wide to bridge. Eventually he was vindicated and attempts were made to rehabilitate him. But all of that was done behind closed doors. In the end, it still didn't get him back into the history of the Church of God or the good graces of those who had turned on him earlier. He remained, to all intents and purposes, an outcast.

It is this that concerns me and provides the dominant motivation for my writing. Brother Tasker was simply too important a part of the events of our collective past to be ignored in this fashion. His conflict with the Missionary Board and the "influential brethren" of the Gospel Trumpet Company was a catalyst—not the only one, but a very important one all the same—in the transition of the Church of God from a narrow, strident, and sectarian little group to the diverse, inclusive, vibrant, and growing community it is generally today.[3]

I'm not at all suggesting that the path of change has been smooth and even, or that the critics have always or necessarily been wrong. They are not now; they were not then. But no telling in what closed-off backwater we might find ourselves today without persons like Brother Tasker, who have been willing to run ahead of the crowd, risking kicks and stones from the rear.

It is important wherever histories get muddled or distorted (whether intentionally or not) to set them straight—and this is a classic case. Both A.D. Khan and Mona Moors Tasker were anxious that this be done in the case of Brother Tasker. A.D. Khan writes, "I note with

---

[3] It can, I think, be documented that the Church of God did not really begin to grow significantly until the come-out doctrine began to go into eclipse. After its first 50 years, the Church had only about 30,000 adult adherents. In the next 50, it increased five-fold. To be sure, numerical growth doesn't tell the whole story, but it is at least an important part of it. When the Church began opening its heart to all born-again Christians everywhere, it had to begin lengthening its "cords" and strengthening its "stakes" in quite dramatic ways. Of course, its many critics within complained of "spiritual decline" and "moral deterioration," turning instead to a "remnant" theology to explain the earlier lack of growth. Small, but pure, they said, just as the Scriptures teach. Perhaps. Perhaps not.

satisfaction . . . that interest is at last being taken to put his life and work in proper perspective. For he was a much misunderstood man, and it is time something was done to rehabilitate his image" (personal letter).

That Brother Tasker was indeed misunderstood is most probable. That he was misjudged and maligned unfairly is likely. That he was a pivotal person in the historical transformation of the Church of God is even more likely. It is not possible, in my view, to trace the historical change that has occurred in our collective life–change that amounts almost to a seismic shift–without looking closely at his influence and contribution. Metamorphosis would eventually have occurred without him, I think, but a different kind of metamorphosis over a much longer period of time. In any event, without the data provided by his story we would have a much more difficult time judging that.

## Church of God Heritage

My Church of God heritage--of which I am deeply appreciative–came to me from Western Canada and the Pacific Northwest of the United States. It has given me a place to feel at home. In the ensuing fifty years, I've become keenly aware–even painfully aware at times--that it is not the only Church of God heritage among us. I say painfully aware because on occasion heritages from other geographical regions of the United States have been (are?) held up and passionately proclaimed as the "true" and only Church of God heritage.

I find this painful, because it is demeaning and exclusionary. Suddenly, I'm on the outside, "a heretic, a rebel, a thing to flout . . ." along with thousands of other fine Christian people, many of whom have loved and nurtured me in the faith. Without their deep commitment to Christ, I would not be who and where I am today. That is simply too sad to dwell on for long.

But it gets me thinking about this problem of heritage. Our heritage is the story handed on to us and, I suppose, the story we hand on to those who follow after us. Each time it is handed on–as we should expect if we actually stopped to think about it–the story is heard a little differently. After even a few generations, the story being told would scarcely be recognized at some points by those who first began to tell it. It is recognizably the same, yet also obviously different.

We, of course, have the advantage of writing and, in many cases, can go back to the original story, trying to figure out as nearly as possible what happened and what was said about it. This is what historians do—or at least are supposed to do. To go back to the beginning and select from the available data merely to prop up a particular heritage is at best misguided and at worst dishonest. It suggests that what actually took place must be carefully tailored, trimmed, and tidied up (history, after all, is a messy and inexact "science") and made to fit the heritage. But historians, must dig out "facts" and at least *try* to let *them* shape the story.

### History and the Heritage Syndrome

It will be helpful at this point, I think, to further explore this distinction between the heritage syndrome and history. While this may seem like an unnecessary diversion, it is really not, since much of my approach to the writing of this particular history is based on that distinction. James W. Loewen, in *Lies Across America: What Our Historic Sites Got Wrong* (1999), best highlights the difference for me.

> "The heritage syndrome," as historian Michael Kammen calls it, is "an impulse to remember what is attractive or flattering and to ignore all the rest." Thus history and heritage are not the same; indeed, the two are often at odds. When Edward Ball, in the 1990s, began to research his family's ownership of slaves, some other members of his family grew upset. While they reveled in the "heritage" of their links to the gentry of the antebellum South, they did not want Bell bringing out what actually happened. The conflict between history and heritage goes still deeper. Too often events that reek of dishonor get abracadabraed into a noble heritage (pp. 41-42).

Thus are persons and events idealized, becoming noble examples to inspire us all. This, Loewen says, "promotes fallacious history." And that is exactly what often results. People whose accomplishments were really quite ordinary or liberally peppered with inconsistency and human foible are remembered as great persons of extraordinary accomplishments, "men of great faith" and purity of motives.

Heritage forgets, not only that they had clay feet, but that they had feet at all. They didn't walk on *terra firma* like the rest of humanity, but somehow above it, not affected by the push and pull of context and circumstance. They are neither *of* their times, nor *ahead of* their times, but *above* the times altogether. And so they become mythic characters. (The Catholic Church often canonizes them and calls them saints. We Protestants are less formal.)

The problem with the heritage syndrome, as I see it, is that it forces us, as Loewen suggests, to recognize only "happy history," "impressive people," events people can "take pride in" (p. 34). Heritage, he notes, is something you feel good about. It tells a "positive" story, a story of struggle and hope and victory, of "heroes" of the past overcoming great handicaps or odds, winning out in the end when it seemed everything was lost.

Who is not inspired by the story of Helen Keller, for example? But how many people—besides careful historians not interested in writing popular inspirational tales—know that Ms. Keller was socially and politically quite radical, supporting trade unions, racial justice and integration, birth control, women's rights—including voting rights—and—oh! the shame of it!—communism (see Loewen, p. 243f)? Most of us don't even *want* to know that. Heritage is much more fun than real history!

## The Loss of Historical Memory

It appears to me that we are in danger of losing our historical memory. What too often passes for history among us is heritage. What we are much too frequently given—at least at the popular level—is "uplifting" stories abstracted from a much larger tapestry of human events, a tapestry full of dark colors as well as bright. These "uplifting stories" in their context often contain that which is anything but uplifting. They do not inspire us to "go and do likewise," but quite the opposite. Indeed, as Robert Reardon lamented in a personal conversation, "I'm tired of whitewashed history." (And so should we all be!)

Part of the problem, as I see it, is our Western *Christian* cultural heritage itself.. Almost from day one, we are taught to be "nice," "positive," "encouraging," "uplifting," thinking and speaking only "whatever is true, whatever is noble, whatever is right, whatever is pure, whatever is lovely, whatever is admirable," or excellent, or praiseworthy–and that from the Apostle Paul, who was himself on some occasions the apostle of "un-nice" (Philippians 4:8, the oft-quoted Christian credo for "nice"–interesting indeed that all of these "nice" qualities get stressed, and "whatever is true" is left out).

Thus, we are not morally trained to think about the opposite of "nice" and to discuss it openly and honestly. For this reason, "Yes, but...." people tend to be unpopular. If for the sake of balance and perspective, not at all to be disagreeable and contrary, these people point out the dark colors in the tapestry that quite change the way the bright colors should be perceived, they will probably spend a lot of time eating lunch alone. They are infected with "un-nice." They are "negative" and "critical." [4]

---

[4] I feel very strongly about this problem. On occasion I have talked to writers and preachers who have given a "sugar-coated" or "whitewashed" account of persons and events within our history. To my great surprise, every now and then, they will admit they know things really didn't happen "exactly" that way. Important details that would have changed the direction of the story were knowingly left out in order not to "cast any negative light" on the persons involved." But," they say, "you really can't tell most people that. It would discourage them, or cause them to turn away from the Church, or to withhold financial support." This desire to be "uplifting and inspiring" is noble, I suppose. But it is not honest. And intellectual honesty, in my view, is not a luxury. It is a requirement for genuine spirituality. Of course, negative or sordid details that do not materially alter a story should be left out. They serve no purpose, except perhaps to

This frequently leads us to produce "whitewashed" history, history with everything extracted except the good, the noble, the uplifting, the inspiring, the beautiful—and in the process extracting also the "whatever is true." Such "historians" (who are really community "bards" singing the praises of great "men" and "miraculous" or "divine" events) could, I suppose, be called "cheerleaders." They are "champions," in the medieval sense of that word, heralds who proclaim the greatness of those they represent—and in the process may turn even rapacious villains into great liberators and heroes. (Or the other way around if you are a Westerner writing a history of Fidel Castro! The historical truth is he was probably a little of each.)

### An Overriding Concern

My concern in writing this life of Brother Tasker is to produce *history*, not the amorphous, context-free, stuff from which heritage is often constructed. For this reason, I go into more contextual detail than is usual in the biographies we have produced in the past. Some may find this a bit tedious, although I hope this will not be the case. But I am convinced that the story must be seen as part of the tapestry into which it is woven if we are to have any chance at all of seeing it correctly.

In writing history, we must argue from what counts among historical researchers and writers of history as "evidence." In our case, the evidence consists of what historians call "primary" documents: letters; diaries; reports; minutes; personal papers; articles; and pamphlets. We have been able to collect much of this material for deposit in Church of God Archives. Without it, the Tasker story would be thin indeed—at some points very thin!

To be sure, not all of the "evidence" needs to be presented—if its omission does not materially alter the story.

---

pass along gossip. Gossip is gossip, not history. But "whatever is true" that would materially alter the story is a part of the story that should be told. Otherwise we have distortion and untruth.

But I've included what I judge to be "representative" evidence, evidence I've felt was necessary to tell the story of Brother Tasker in his primary context, that is, the Church of God. Without this, I could not see myself as writing genuine history, but trying to create heritage.

You may wish I'd told the story less completely. I have, in fact, not included a good deal that interests me personally, not because it doesn't constitute historical fact, but because it doesn't contribute significantly to our story. What I have included is, as best I can determine, what most likely happened. I've felt no need to withhold what I see as important facts, simply out of deference to our heritage. That is certainly no way to "set the record straight."

I realize this is a risk. To tell the story fairly and honestly, I must open both myself and Brother Tasker to public view (in some sense, the kind of biography I'm writing here is also autobiography). In doing this, it is quite easy to open oneself to misunderstanding, harsh judgment, even rejection. But to restore Brother Tasker to our collective historical memory and secure for him the place in our history books he deserves is a risk worth the taking.

Another risk, however, may be even greater. That is, the risk that this whole endeavor will be simply ignored. What does it matter who George Pease Tasker was? What does it matter what happened back there? Then was then; now is now. We weren't there and had no hand in his judgment and dismissal. Perhaps it was deserved; perhaps not. But it changes absolutely nothing in the present–which is where we should be living anyway. This is the historical apathy we find nowadays throughout church and society, a kind of ho-hum, so-what mentality.

Some of this—as seriously misguided as it is—is, of course, understandable. A large percentage of Church of God adherents today do not have Church of God roots of any kind. They have come from other traditions (not as come-outers, but for a variety of other reasons, not the least of which is geographical convenience–the same reason many former Church of God adherents no longer attend Church of God congregations). Their root system is firmly "evangelical" (forget the holiness tradition) and they find nothing seriously objectionable in Church of God polity or doctrine (although our amillenialism seems a bit weird to some of them, who occasionally try their best to correct our unfortunate oversight).

Since Church of God congregations–particularly larger ones–in many places are now generically "evangelical," being overtly Church of God is no longer "in." A kind of amorphous evangelical tree has been grafted onto Church of God roots. Many non-Church of God clergy persons (but certainly church of God, as Brother Tasker would insist) can feel quite comfortable pastoring these churches. Church of God history is generally only of passing interest to them–if they have any interest in it at all.

But, for many of us, Church of God heritage is what defines us. My concern is that this heritage be as fully *historically* informed as possible. Without that, we shall merely be deluding ourselves that whatever is good, whatever is beautiful, whatever is positive, whatever is noble and uplifting is all there is in our past.

And so we shall be tempted to go on covering up the inadequacies and blunders from which we might learn valuable lessons. Rather than rejoicing in the wrong, or relishing the uncovering of it, we learn instead to *lament* it– not *condemn* it--and see to it that it no longer happens among us–in that form, at least. Much in the story I will tell you needs to be lamented in just this fashion. As one of the early players in that drama cried out: "Lets never let it happen again that personal ambition should run so wild. Let it not happen again in our fellowship." Only by correcting our heritage with history can we see to it that it does not.

A new millenium has now begun and it is high time the story of George Pease Tasker is told among us and in the generations to come. We need to hear it in these days when we are tempted to repeat some of the mistakes of our forebears in this fellowship. But it seems that repeating mistakes is something most of us are rather good at. Those who are poor readers–or no readers at all–of their own history tend to do that.

Perhaps we've grown up now and can accept facts that

were too hard to swallow by those much closer to the events that removed Brother Tasker from among us. We cannot, from this point in the course of events, be too harshly critical of them. We were not there and were not involved in the heat of the battle. We cannot–as thoroughly as we may search the available documents and as carefully as we may try to reconstruct the context–know what they knew and fear what they feared. Their "shoes" are their "shoes," not ours.

Therefore, if history collides with the heritage we've been bequeathed, we of this generation should finally be able to handle that without coming unstuck. Nowadays, we don't label friends and colleagues in the faith as heretics and excommunicate them, or engage in acrimonious verbal battles and name-calling. Well, almost never. Not as often?

## A Literary Disclaimer

It's usual among educators to write *formally*. We are not supposed to use contractions (such as "it's," for example); write non-sentences (such as the two at the end of the last paragraph); begin sentences with conjunctions ("and" or "but"); end sentences with prepositions (which, as Winston Churchill once said tongue-in-cheek, is "a practice up with which we ought not to put"); or use "that most terrible of all pronouns," first person singular "I".

I have deliberately and cheerfully violated all of the writing rules I have taught for years in my graduate research and writing courses as wrong. Why? In the first place, because I'm not writing a book for educators, who have been rigorously trained in the academic traditions of formality and are not terribly comfortable out of them. And, in the second place, because formal writing does not seem to me appropriate to the personalized kind of biography I'm writing here. I'm telling a story and story language seems to me to "strike the ear" much more satisfactorily than the usually more laborious prose of formal writing.

I have chosen to write for those whose literacy is more ordinary and less concerned about all of the formal niceties of grammar and syntax. In my everyday life, I try to avoid split infinitives and double negatives and other similar linguistic barbarities–and have learned that "she" is a subject and "her" an object of a verb or a preposition. But, while trying to avoid slangy and grammatically crude language, I really don't "talk like a book" in my normal conversation. Most people consider that affected. And rightly so.

Therefore, I have knowingly and purposefully adopted a conversational style of writing. I want that to be reflected in the prose that appears on paper. Formal language is not nearly as good as informal language at doing that. On this matter, I've come to believe my own rhetoric (always a present danger): "learn the rules well, then break them creatively." I'm comfortable writing this way. And, I suspect, many readers are just as comfortable reading the same way.

## Organization of The Material

I have not organized the material for this book in any recognizable chronological fashion. Therefore, I will, on occasion, hopscotch back and forth in my telling of the story. I personally dislike the "telephone book" approach (names, dates, and places) to the writing of history. Not that such biographical information is not important. Not at all! That may constitute the bare facts, the essential skeletal data, as it were, but skeletons belong under flesh and blood, not out in the open parading around as real persons–or real history.

I've organized the available material around six over-arching questions, questions which serve as chapter headings. Who was this man? What was he? What went wrong when everything went wrong? What were his theological views? Where did it all end? Where does it all lead? No inescapable inner logic determines such an approach. I have no compelling reason for doing this, other than the fact that this arrangement appeals to me.

Chapters 1, 2, and 5 consist largely of the presentation of the biographical data themselves. Chapters 3 and 4 are more interpretive in nature–and thus, perhaps, more controversial, particularly chapter 3, "What Went Wrong

When Everything Went Wrong." But it is in chapter 6, the so-what? chapter, that controversy truly comes into its own—as you will see.

I'm well aware that some may neither agree with nor like my particular interpretation of the data. It is not my purpose to generate controversy simply for the sake of controversy. The story that I myself am at this point in my life compels my interpretation. It is not really possible for me finally to interpret the data other than I have done. If that produces controversy, so be it.

But, then, I suppose, a book that is not controversial in some measure at least, merely reiterating–however learnedly and cleverly–what we already all know and believe, probably need not be written at all. In fact, it may be held to constitute a grievous crime against trees. I hope I shall not prove to be guilty of that.

### Acknowledgments

Before beginning our story, it is appropriate here, I think, to acknowledge those who have given help and encouragement in this undertaking. Initial encouragement in 1979 came from Robert Reardon, John D. Crose, and John W.V. Smith. Latterly, I have gotten a great deal of support from friends, colleagues, and family. My wife, Ruth, has taken an unflagging interest in this project and has made many helpful suggestions, as well as doing the final proof-reading. Barry Callen, Editor of Anderson University Press has gone much further than the "second mile" to see that this book reaches the light of day. And many thanks to my long-time friend and colleague, Merle Strege, for his excellent and insightful Foreword.

A number of friends have given invaluable help in the collection of Tasker materials and memorabilia. I owe much to Robert Reardon and David Davis for providing key materials. But my special gratitude goes to Irene Engst, long-time Africa missionary and good friend of Mona Moors Tasker, for her "collecting" in the Penticton area and for putting me onto new sources for materials. Such colleagues and friends are indeed a great treasure. This book would be much poorer without them.

# Chapter 1

## WHO WAS THIS MAN?

It's not easy to write such a chapter as this. Brother Tasker did not talk much about himself or his personal life. He was such an unusually Christ-centered man that it would likely never have occurred to him that later generations might want to read his personal story. I think I remember something about "he must increase, but I must decrease."

Therefore, I've had to scour the countryside, shaking every promising bush–and some unpromising ones–to collect biographical information. Thus many of my sources are secondary, but, I think, reliable in the main–although a few inconsistencies and disagreements have surfaced. Persons such as Mona Moors Tasker, Aurelius D. Khan, John D. Crose, and R.R. Byrum are, as a result, my principle informants.

### Basic Biographical Facts

The man we know as George Pease Tasker was born George Pease, in Winnemucca, Nevada, on October 8, 1872, one of four children born to Lucius Curtis Pease and his wife (who is unnamed in the documents, as the custom of the day often dictated). The children were orphaned when George was 13 months old. George, but none of the other children–contrary to a couple of sources that state otherwise–was adopted by a maternal aunt who lived in Montreal, Quebec. He grew up knowing only the Taskers as his parents and Montreal as his home.

Montreal was certainly "no mean city." By 1892, when George Pease Tasker was 20 years of age, it was 250 years old and a prosperous, progressive, and cosmopolitan city. Between 1850 and the time of Brother Tasker's birth, Montreal had transformed itself into a noted metropolis of large mechanized factories, import businesses, banks, insurance companies, office buildings, cathedrals, libraries, and educational institutions. Because of its extensive railway links to all of North America and its large port, Montreal soon became a busy center of international life and trade. In some sense, the world flowed through Montreal.

It was also a noted center of culture and the arts. In addition to its dominant French-speaking population, Catholic and conservative in culture, Montreal boasted a large English-speaking minority—who certainly dominated the economic and social life of the city. Predominantly British, this minority was largely Protestant. And among the Protestants, Scottish Presbyterians, such as the Taskers, were quite common.

The Taskers appear to have been very godly people, though doubtless not in the eyes of the Evening Light saints with whom George Pease Tasker later aligned himself. He speaks of a mother's "fervent prayers" and of godly training and of his father as "an honored elder" in St. Paul's Presbyterian Church in Montreal (*Gospel Trumpet*, Nov 17, 1921). He does not say what his father did for a living, but he seems to have been socially prominent—at least within the minority Protestant community—and to have lived in comfortable circumstances. At some point, I think I recall Brother Tasker using the phrase "well-to-do."

George Pease Tasker was likely quite well educated for his day, having spent one year in prestigious McGill University in Montreal, before apprenticing as a diamond setter, a trade he worked at for 5 years. C.E. Brown asserts that the young Tasker was very unhappy at McGill. Perhaps he heard him say this at some point—one of those off-the-cuff remarks we all make without much thought, which we probably wouldn't make if we thought about them. It is certainly not documented anywhere. Given Brother Tasker's obvious intelligence and intellectual gifts, I really can't think why. Perhaps he was simply bored— something that often happens to very bright students in academic settings that are too conventional in their approaches to education.

What is certain is that Brother Tasker was a well-read man. Some of the books in his library were classics in historical, missiological, and biblical studies. Near the end of his life, he contacted me, asking me to come and see him. He told me that he wanted me to have first pick of his library. One of the first books I chose was Theodore Zahn's *Introduction to the New Testament,* a limited edition one-volume work–and prized by collectors of biblical studies books. He laughed with delight and said, "Ah, my boy, you know a good book when you see one. Adam Miller has been trying for years to get that book from me." That book is still in my possession  after 43 years–15 of those in East Africa–and is now sitting prominently on the book shelf opposite me as I write.

From a purely social standpoint, it might be argued that his fondness for good books was one of his failings. Mona Moors Tasker said, "He was a constant reader. If he was not in deep discussion over a theological point with someone, he would be off in a corner with a book. He had no interest in social chit chat."  Being educated may or may not have much to do with formal schooling. We've all known people with doctoral degrees who are not educated. They've never learned how to learn–and are not much interested in doing so in any case.

But Brother Tasker was an educated man, something he spent a lifetime in achieving. It was the second thing people meeting him for the first time noticed about him. The first was his Christ-centeredness. Brother H.C. Heffren, founder and long-time editor of *The Gospel Contact*, the official paper of the Church of God in Western Canada, had this to say of him: "He showed himself cultured and refined and with great intellectual genius. His was no ordinary concept of the Word, but he was 'mighty in the Scriptures . . . He could tear into shreds the arguments of the modernists'" (*The Gospel Contact*, May 23, 1958).

But, back to McGill. McGill University , endowed by a wealthy merchant, James McGill, was chartered in 1821 as a private, non-denominational school of higher learning in the English language. Three noted Protestant Colleges engaging in the training of ministers and missionaries later affiliated with it: the Anglican Diocesan College; United Theological College; and Presbyterian College. This mix of liberal arts, medicine, science, and theology was a heady environment that would have had considerable effect on any person of the young Tasker's keen intellect and intelligence who was part of it for any length of time.

George Pease Tasker would thus have been exposed to a cosmopolitan world of books and music and libraries, as well as French culture and language, something the French in Quebec have always seen to with pride and passion. It is unlikely that young George would have escaped this influence, even if his family had been inclined to do so.

So what do we have? An urbane and polished citizen of a city steeped in two great cultures, British and French, Protestant and Catholic. He was also part of a deeply-rooted "evangelical" religious tradition, the child of a comfortable home and circumstances. He knew who he was and what he was capable of. Small wonder that he was so self-confident and open-minded about so many things.

Who George Pease Tasker was certainly determined the course of his life and ministry in the Church of God (Anderson, Indiana). He was a leader, a teacher, an intellectual force, a devout Christian, a deeply spiritual man, a "presence," as John D. Crose described him to me. Some men and women, by their station and demeanor, *demand* attention and respect. Brother Tasker *commanded* it, without willing that it be so. Such people do not need to engage in self-promotion—something he neither liked nor practiced. It was not "Christ-like."

Even though he was a small man physically—probably not more than five feet three or four inches tall, if even that, and slender in build—Brother Tasker was a giant of a man inwardly. He was large-minded and warm-spirited in ways that made him stand out in any setting. Had he been born forty years later, he may have survived in the Church of God and been an outstanding preacher, teacher, and leader among us. But, then, he may not have been what he was: an extraordinary man in extraordinary circumstances.

24

## Conversion and Early Ministry

While it appears that Brother Tasker had been reared as a devout and practicing Christian, as a young man he was in a state of spiritual and mental turmoil until well into his twenties. He refers to it as "a seven year search for inward peace and victory over sin." Here are his own words:

> . . . my soul was flooded with his great salvation. In purpose and intention, I had long before renounced the devil and given myself up to God the best I knew. I belonged to him, no doubt, though I must confess that fear of sin's desert had been the controlling motive in my consecration, and not the Savior's love. I was too self-occupied to realize that. But now, what passed between my soul and its Lord in those never-to-be-forgotten days when his love and grace were first revealed in me, I have never been able to tell. Then it was that I really passed out of self into Christ, out of death into life, out of darkness into light, out of bondage into liberty. Hallelujah! *(Gospel Trumpet,* Nov 17, 1921).

Brother Tasker was then 23 years of age and living in Philadelphia. He never did say when he moved there or what he was doing. In those days, children born in the United States could move back to the U.S. before age 21 and thus retain their American citizenship. Perhaps that prompted the move. Since Brother Tasker did have a United States passport, that may have been the case. But, again, we have no way of knowing for certain. We may also assume, I think, that he was likely still engaged in his diamond setting trade, at least for a while, but neither is that by any means certain.

Within a year—perhaps only a few months, we cannot be sure—he moved to Chicago. Here he worked in an evangelical mission of some sort, whether full-time or part-time we do not know. Nor do we know how he supported himself during this period. What we do know is that it is here he first came into contact with people of the Evening Light. Again, his own story in his own words:

About eighteen months after my conversion I received light on believer's baptism from my study of the Scriptures, and was immersed in accordance with Christ's command. I was in Chicago at the time, having gone there in my search for a people who discerned the body of Christ, to which my own eyes had already been opened one evening while reading 1 Cor. 12:12, 13. That vision of the oneness of those in Christ spoiled me for sectarianism forever, and while it was a divine revelation to me individually, I felt sure that the Lord must have a *people* somewhere who *as a body* had the same vision and were devoted to the whole will of God. Such a people, I felt, were my people; so I deliberately set out to find them (*Gospel Trumpet*, Nov 17, 1921, author's italics).

A few months later, and presumably still in Chicago, while listening to a preacher from India, Brother Tasker consecrated his life completely to the service of God and "received the Holy Spirit." This was a second great turning point in his life. He writes of this experience as follows:

Some four months after my baptism, and following a period of much earnest inquiry and prayer for the fullness of God, Christ was so revealed to my heart as its intended and everlasting portion that the long-desired complete consecration was induced, in the experience of which, on Nov. 12, 1897, I received the blessed Comforter, the Holy Ghost, "the promise of the Father." The particular promise that gave me faith for the purifying baptism was Ezek. 36:25, 26 and–remarkable fact–it was a native of India whose preaching God used to bring me into spiritual Canaan. Never shall I forget that night when the Holy Spirit of my God and his Christ came into my very nature to *abide*. This may not be theological language, but it is just

the way I should express it if left to the choice of
my own words, and it was all by simple faith in
God's promise. Blessed be his name (*GT*, Nov 17,
1921).

Probably shortly thereafter, that is, in late 1897, two
brethren of the Church of God—or Church in the Evening
Light, as Brother Tasker phrases it—George L. Cole and
Gorham Tufts (who ran the Open Door Mission in
Chicago), visited the mission in which he worked. He says,
"I felt peculiarly drawn to them in spirit and later visited
them . . . ." Two other "saints in the evening light," Joseph
and Emma Johnson, also visited the mission and were
probably the ones who gave him his first *Gospel Trumpet*.

Here Brother Tasker makes a very interesting criticism
of the *Trumpet*—and, remember, it was published in that
very same *Trumpet*. It is also rather lengthy, but Brother
Tasker was a gifted writer and it is delightful to read his
prose.

One reads a good deal about how the paper
has led this one and that one into the precious light
of full salvation and the unity of God's people, and
where such is the case we might well rejoice. Truth,
however, requires the confession that there are
also cases where, on account of the narrowness
that characterized many of the writings of those
days, the paper had a different effect. I do not think
that the *Gospel Trumpet* as it then was would have
won me. It was *the love and spirit of Christ I felt in
the brethren themselves* that drew me and bound
me to them. On the whole the paper itself, aside
from some of the expositions of Scripture,
especially upon the subjects of the two covenants
and the millenium, was a real handicap in my case;
although I could sincerely say that the principles for
which it contended were those of my own heart.
But Brother Warner's hymns—how they fitted and
expressed the feelings of my soul! I sent for a copy
of the song-book *Echoes From Glory* and sang
those songs constantly. I had found my people

(*Gospel Trumpet,* Nov 17, 1921, author's italics).

He had, indeed, found his people. And he was not long in joining them in evangelistic and teaching ministry. When we hear of him again, he is in Ontario, Canada, preaching Christ and the Evening Light. From the beginning, what really mattered was that one preached Christ. It was okay to preach Evening Light, but that must never be allowed to stand above and overshadow the Christ. The Christ-first principle was basic to the person he had become; no movement or church could be allowed to displace that.

Here the record is confused and confusing. Some sources say one thing; some say another. Brother Tasker himself says nothing, other than "I was working in Ontario at the time." An Anderson University School of Theology student thesis says that in 1898 Brother Tasker and Harry W. Nelson started a work at Grand Valley, or Peepabun, Ontario (Beverley C. Anderson, *A History of the Church of God in Ontario 1882-1955).* John W.V. Smith says it was in 1899 (*The Quest for Holiness and Unity* 1980:107). Another source, not named, but on record, declares that it was John Blaney who actually founded the church in Peepabun. And so it goes. Life would be so much simpler for us historical types if Brother Tasker had just told us what actually happened.

A part of the problem is the Gorham Tufts story. Brother Tasker does say that he was working in Ontario when Gorham Tufts wrote to him urging him to accompany him to India. This, it turns out, was not to carry famine relief funds to India, as our School of Theology student seems to assume—Tufts had done that in 1897 as the official representative of the Gospel Trumpet Company—but constituted an independent effort to engage in missionary work. So when was it that Tufts wrote to Brother Tasker? Probably 1899, since Brother Tasker himself says that he traveled to India eight years later accompanied by H.A. Brooks, that is, in 1907.

All of this means that our School of Theology student was probably at least partially right and the work in Peepabun was started in 1898, not in 1899. How high is this on the possibility-probability scale, which is really all historians have to work with? Much more, I think, than half way between the two. Probably. The problem in dating events for which no months are given is that years have Januaries and then they have Decembers. The confusion has led some to choose one date, some the other.

We do not know much about these early days of Brother Tasker's involvement in the churches in Ontario. At least until the Gospel Trumpet Company re-established itself in Anderson, Indiana, in 1906, he continued to do evangelistic and teaching work in Ontario. He had many good friends there, friends whom he valued highly and with whom he did his best to communicate over the years.

We do not know if he ever returned to Montreal. His parents may have been very bitterly opposed to their son's new affiliation–or so I have heard or read somewhere. Given their probable religious convictions and their social position, I can't imagine them being overjoyed. Let's face it. For all the world, these self-styled "Saints in the Evening Light" must have seemed to those of traditional, conventional Christian convictions and commitments a radical, fanatical, narrow, excessively dogmatic, and ignorant little sect located somewhere out close to the cultic fringe. How incomprehensible, how embarrassing it must have all seemed to persons like the Taskers.

But the notion of such bitter opposition may be derived, as in other cases, from oral tradition of uncertain origin. That the Taskers were not happy with their son's choice is highly probable. Mona Moors Tasker did say that "he went against his parents wishes when he associated with the small Church of God congregations and finally left Canada for the States" (Moundsville, West Virginia, I assume, where the Gospel Trumpet Company was located from 1898 to 1906). She goes on to say that a sister, Ella, grew up in the United States, but lived with them for a while in Valley View Lodge in Penticton toward the end of her life. The second sister is not mentioned. A brother Lute, who also grew up in the eastern U.S., became "a well-known artist and writer."

Brother Tasker himself did not say much about his family, either the Taskers or the Peases. Of course, the "lost diaries" may have contained references. Who knows?

But he had joined a new family, a family to which he gave his devotion and loyalty. From then on, their fortunes would be his. If his parents rejected him—even though I tend to doubt that they did—he would have counted that loss as gain in Christ. As I've said, perhaps monotonously, he was an unusually Christ-centered man. He did not speak much of himself.

## On to Moundsville

It is most likely, then, that sometime in 1900 Brother Tasker joined the saints at Moundsville, West Virginia. He was 28 years of age and a refined and polished gentleman, someone who stood out in any group, and particularly in a group such as those gathered in the Trumpet home in Moundsville—hardly a center of culture and sophistication.

It is interesting to speculate about how the Saints must have appeared to him. They were, for the most part, from the lower classes, the majority of them probably of rural or small town origin (no demerit in itself, to be sure, otherwise I am seriously demerited myself). That usually meant, among other things, rather limited formal public schooling. Their dress, speech, and manners were generally those of country and small town people. Their lifestyle in the Trumpet family was basically that of the relatively poor, food and accommodations were quite plain and simple, and the amenities of urban life so few they were virtually non-existent.

It is, I think, an often observed historical and social fact that those of "higher" social class and cultural attainments either are, or assume they are, the natural leaders and teachers of the "lower" classes. Brother Tasker, however, was too Christ-centered to think himself better than others. More privileged—much more. But not better. He was, I think, quite graciously accepting of others, no matter what their background or station in life. His missionary record in India from the very beginning seems to speak of that.

In any event, he appeared in Moundsville, joined the "family," and went to work in the business department. He was quite probably not formally trained in business administration, so far as we know–his time at McGill had been spent in "Applied Science," whatever that was–but he was a very bright and adaptable man and seemed to be able to master whatever needed doing. Thus, he would have taken to his assignment quite easily and with enthusiasm. His station in life and innate abilities gave him a healthy self-confidence.

That was soon evident. This was no ordinary man. According to C.E. Brown, in *When The Trumpet Sounded,* Brother Tasker took "an active and prominent place in the work almost from the beginning" (1951:203). Brother Tasker would. He was simply that kind of a man.

Interestingly, it is from C.E. Brown alone that we learn that Brother Tasker had "for many years" been active in leadership in the YMCA. Was that what he was doing in Philadelphia? Strange that he should not bother to mention it–not even in the information he supplied to Thaddeus Neff for Neff's 1956 publication, *Our Missionaries.* But, as his widow, Mona Moors Tasker, commented to me, "My G.P. was never one to blow his own horn." If Brother Brown is right, then Brother Tasker's experience in administration and leadership would have brought him quickly to the forefront at Moundsville.

Even so, "many years" may be something of an over-reach. I should think it could have been only a year or two at most. I'm thinking about his age and his long period of formal education and apprenticeship. He certainly may have been involved at some point with the YMCA–that rings a bell in my mind and could be from something he himself said or wrote–but hardly, I think, for "many years." After all, he was not that long out of his teens when he appeared in Chicago. Since Brother Brown does not document his claim, I'm somewhat inclined to doubt it. Brother Tasker did nonetheless appear to have innate leadership and administrative abilities. In that, Brother Brown was correct.

Besides, Brother Tasker's intellectual gifts were simply too great for him not to be noticed. Brown comments that Tasker "showed himself one of the most intellectual men in our fellowship." He continues: "I remember that in 1906 he told me he was interested in Delitzsh's *Biblical*

*Psychology,* a book which few other men [read, "none"] among us would have cared to read at that time . . . ."

### And Anderson

When, in 1906, the *Gospel Trumpet* publishing house was moved from Moundsville, West Virginia to Anderson, Indiana, Brother Tasker was one of the first to move with it. By this time, he was doing considerable writing and teaching, work he had quite quickly fallen into in Moundsville. He appears to have assumed an even more prominent role in Anderson. Harold Phillips notes in *Miracle of Survival* that G.P. Tasker, one of 12 men, was a charter member of the new not-for-profit corporation formed in Indiana (1979:107).

His stature in the Gospel Trumpet Company is evident in a letter written in 1910 by A. L. Byers to F.G. Smith, who was in Lacota, Michigan at the time. Byers writes: "Dear Brother: Your MS, 'Evolution of Christianity,' is on its return from Bro. Tasker, who writes and expresses his approval of it. Its acceptance by the Pub. Com. is therefore practically assured, tho' Bro. Teasley has not yet read it." What a telling statement! For a small man, Brother Tasker seems to have carried a lot of weight.

Here Brother Tasker, among other responsibilities, assumed pastoral leadership of the Trumpet Home–or so R.R. Byrum stated in an interview. He may also, from time to time, have occupied the *Gospel Trumpet* Editor's Chair during long absences of E.E. Byrum. I cannot document this, however. But I have heard it from at least two generally reliable oral sources. It makes sense. His abilities in this area appear to have outshone anyone else's. If Brother Tasker thought Christ would be honored by anything he was asked to do, he did it gladly and with boundless energy.

About a year and a half after moving to Anderson, that is, in 1907, Brother Tasker, accompanied by H.A. Brooks, left Anderson on a missions trip that lasted for twenty months. This included Britain and Egypt and eventually India where he spent nine months. The trip was cut short by his serious illness in India. Brothers Tasker and Brooks returned to Anderson in 1909, accompanied by John A.D. Khan, founder and apostle of the Church of God in India.

That year, Brother Tasker writes, was a "memorable" year. "It was the birth of our Foreign Missionary Board and other important activities, and the larger vision came to many" (*Gospel Trumpet*, Nov 17, 1921). He was surely one of the architects and first members of this group, officially designated as The Missionary Committee–of the Gospel Trumpet Company, it should be added, even though it was established by "common consent" of Church of God ministers meeting at Anderson. Brother Tasker was also one of the leading lights responsible for the birth of the *Missionary Herald* and was Associate Editor of this monthly magazine designed to promote within the Church of God  the cause of world missionary endeavor–a cause that was increasingly his passion.

On February 14, 1910, Brother Tasker was married to Minnie. B. Criswell, whom he had known for some time. He describes her simply as "one like-minded with myself." According to Mack M. Caldwell, one of my former professors, in an interview many years ago, both Minnie and her sister, Jessie Criswell, were at Moundsville. They were his aunts. He also knew Brother Tasker and had a high regard for him. He was, Brother Caldwell said, "a presence, influential, sophisticated, intellectual, culturally ahead." He thought the marriage was a very happy one, even though no offspring resulted.

R.R. Byrum had great respect and affection for Minnie Criswell Tasker. He says, "Minnie Criswell became the spiritual companion and guide of my wife Bessie in her early work as Editor of the children's Sunday School papers when she was around the age of 19 or 20. To be Minnie's associate was to be her follower, and to make life useful to others in prayer and service" (interview). Minnie's was "a beautiful and dedicated life." Brother Tasker would have agreed wholeheartedly with that.

### New York City and Onward

Shortly after their marriage, the Taskers moved to New York City where Brother Tasker was to assist in the teaching and preaching work of the New York Missionary Home. John W.V. Smith writes at some length about this Home:

> Despite their similarities, each of the missionary homes was distinctive and many of them developed unique special ministries. The one in New York City, for instance, became the departure and return point for all the movement's trans-Atlantic travelers and missionaries. These sojourners often stayed for a while to assist in the city ministry. Under the capable leadership of such persons as D. Otis Teasley, George P. Tasker, C.J. Blewitt, and Axchie A. Bolitho, they developed a rather comprehensive program of meetings in various sections of the city and among the immigrant groups in this great cosmopolitan "gateway to the nation." They sponsored three big events each year, a Spring convention, a summer tent campaign during July and August, and a Christmas week convention. Most significantly, they developed a formalized training program for workers. The "New York Bible Training School," as this part of the work was called, . . . offered "exceptional opportunities for personal work, visitation and contact with all nationalities" (1980:234).

I think I would not be wrong if I were to say, "I know who taught the Bible courses." This had for years been Brother Tasker's passion and certainly was in line with his unusual teaching abilities. In Moundsville, at the request of R.R. Byrum and another young man, he began a Bible class for young men. It soon attracted more than 50 young people. He was, Byrum concludes, "the one person who gave me the idea of serious, systematic Bible study." In India, so I was told there, Brother Tasker was "a noted Bible teacher," particularly after the "Painful Separation."

It was in New York that the Taskers agreed that India was to be their field of ministry from that point in their lives onward. (Most missionaries in those days thought of missionary service as a *career*, not a temporary venture or stepping-stone to something "higher.") However, Brother Tasker–if not Sister Tasker–had been heading there for much of his adult life and perhaps even long before that, thanks to the godly influence of a mother who seems to have had a heart for missions. It seems this was destined from the beginning, but it took a lot of years for the fullness of time to come. Now 40 years of age, he was finally ready to take up his missionary calling–and she hers. Both were uniquely suited and prepared for what was to come.

For the next 34 years, "Mother India"—as many Indians designate their homeland—was to be Brother Tasker's home. And it was to prove to be Sister Tasker's home for all time. Their commitment to Christ and the gospel and their love for India combined powerfully to keep them in India when most others would probably have surrendered and returned to their own countries of origin.

Brother Tasker had, so he believed, experienced an irrevocable calling from God to pour out his life in India. Had this not been the case, he would have left India for good following the Painful Separation from the Missionary Board of the Church of God. His sense of "call," if anything, increased as the years went by. It was that "call" that defined and shaped his life from that point on, making him the missionary he was to become.

## Chapter 2

## WHAT WAS HE?

To be sure, it is not easy to separate *who* a person is from *what* that person is. In fact, it may not be possible at all. The who and the what of any person's life at any point are so intertwined that you can't be sure you've gotten hold of this strand or that. Who you are, that is your character, determines in large measure what you do, so perhaps more attention should be given to character than to doing–rather backward to what our society seems to believe nowadays.

In this sense, *who* Brother Tasker was in his character was *what* he was in his life and ministry. He was no actor on a large stage, skillfully playing a part, but a fully integrated man centered in Christ. He could not dissimulate. That is, he could not hide what he thought, believed, and felt. Pretense and sham were abhorrent to him. He was neither complicated nor devious. In other words, what you saw was what you got.

While that is to be admired, we must also recognize that it has its limits. Openness and directness, as important as they are to good character–among those of us of European descent–if pushed far enough can too easily become bluntness. Brother Tasker was often blunt and that created problems, particularly with his Indian colleagues for whom such openness and directness did not constitute a virtue. A.D. Khan speaks of Brother Tasker's "forthright and impulsive manner, something which in India tends to be regarded as unworthy of a true prophet."

This, combined with his impatience, often got him into hot water with others or resulted in his own embarrassment. It was not too uncommon for him to leap first and look and painfully regret later–as he surely did in relation to the Missionary Board. But, then, who among us hasn't been guilty of this kind of exercise? Acting on impulse before carefully weighing possible consequences has long worked incredible mischief among us. Brother Tasker could, on occasion, break out into some truly Pauline prose in expressing his scorn of those who he believed were perverting scriptural truth, or defying logic and reason–and then often regret having been so impulsive and hasty.

Brother Tasker wore many "hats" in his long career, spanning at least fifty years or more. After all, he had not retired from ministry in India until he was 74. He was administrator, preacher, pastor, evangelist, teacher, scholar, writer, and, above all, a missionary, serving in India from 1912 to 1946–for almost two-thirds of that time as an independent, self-supporting missionary. He considered himself to be Church of God, but had been, by official Missionary Board action, cut off from the community and the friends he loved.

But more of that later. Here I want to deal with three inter-connected phases of what Brother Tasker was: first, preacher and teacher; secondly, scholar and writer; and thirdly, missionary. The bulk of this chapter will be devoted to his missionary career. I didn't know him as a missionary–except a retired one–but I did know him as preacher, teacher, writer, and scholar, activities which he continued with great gusto from the time he returned to Canada from India until his death twelve years later.

## Preacher and Teacher

In the early days of the Church of God, Brother Tasker was a noted speaker and lecturer.[1] According to R.R.

---

[1] Literary evidence from the earliest years of his association with "the saints" indicates that he was noted both for his preaching ability and his spiritual leadership. Late in January 1906, on the eve of the move to Anderson of the small vanguard who would ready things for the main body who were to follow later, Noah H. Byrum read a poem to the gathered "family" which he had written for the occasion. It is entitled, "Our Anderson Home." His characterization of Brother Tasker, one of the vanguard, is instructive indeed: "*Then following next is a brother who goes for*

Byrum, Brother Tasker "was to the church then what Dale Oldham is today." He was highly articulate and possessed natural rhetorical skills. His cultured background, education, and mastery of the English language were quite evident in his preaching.

Brother Tasker was perhaps something of an unconscious "showman" in his preaching style–or so it must have seemed to those who did not know him well. As a young Christian and aspiring minister of the Gospel, I was deeply impressed by all of the physical activity in which he engaged while preaching. He would become quite excited, moving about, gesturing hugely, and jumping around with surprising agility and energy–and he was certainly no young man then.

Almost all of those in the Church of God in India who remembered Brother Tasker spoke of his preaching ability, his "anointing," his clear and logical presentation of "the truth," and especially his jumping ability. When he became excited, he would leap into the air, often shouting "Hallelujah!" When he preached in the church in which I served as pastor, one of the elders laughingly described him as being "as agile as a mountain goat." Brother Tasker was past 83 at the time and could still jump a foot off the floor.

I do not mean to suggest here that his preaching style was calculated theatre. His joy in preaching the Gospel, his love for the truth as he understood it, simply overcame him, causing physical response that was, if nothing else, quite entertaining, to say the least. But it was surely difficult not to listen, and to go to sleep–the ultimate refuge of the disengaged mind–was just not generally possible without determined effort.

Brother Tasker fit into the Indian context very well. I

---

*their spiritual good; He's always so happy and merry, He would not feel bad if he could. We'll miss his bright face in the pulpit, When once he has gone on his way; But we'll pray for our dear Brother Tasker, At the closing of each busy day."* Not terribly good poetry, but the sentiment is plain. (Others in the vanguard included Enoch Byrum, manager and administrator and Noah H. Byrum, treasurer and bookkeeper.)

discovered at the South India campmeeting that long sermons were the order of the day. After an hour, P.V. Jacob usually had to take over from me, especially in the evenings when I had already preached in two other services during the day. Good preachers carried on for at least an hour and a half–even longer if they were really good. Brother Tasker was really good.

That was fine for India. The only problem was that he tended to continue in Canada what he had been practicing in India for the previous 35 years and probably without repeating himself, as most of us would tend to do–which is no great problem for those of us who have learned to say the same thing in a great many different ways. Speaking briefly, "that he may hear who runneth" was not Brother Tasker's strong side.

He was a popular campmeeting and convention speaker, whether in North America or India, but, apart from his ministry in the Gospel Trumpet Home in Anderson, he never served as a pastor, although he did so for several years in India. We will have more to say in Chapter 5 about that. His work in Ontario between 1899 and 1905 was evangelistic in nature–a sort of Pauline coming and going. His was not a pastoral calling.

Second only to his love of preaching was his passion for teaching, particularly Bible teaching. Wherever he stayed for any length of time, he gave Bible lectures. According to my respondents in India, he was noted far and wide as an unusual Bible teacher, lecturing wherever he was invited. And, as Mona Moors Tasker said, "He was invited, from Meghalaya in the north to South India." She went on to say, "He was always a Bible teacher, wherever he was."

A number of his lecture series were published and circulated, primarily in India. Unfortunately, most of these are no longer to be found. He covered an array of subjects, including, among others, God, the church, the second coming of Christ, the sanctified life, the epistle to the Romans, and divorce and remarriage.

## Scholar and Writer

Brother Tasker was a scholarly man. He read widely and deeply, delving into areas of study and thought that most of his peers in the movement would have found daunting. Popular Christian books were of little abiding interest to him. He thought them to be shallow and predictable, circling endlessly around a few fundamental truths and a great many mistruths.

This does not mean that he was not aware of what was being written in the field of "pop theology," or never read any of it. His arguments against much of it indicated that he did. He was a scholar and scholars tend to read even that which argues what they themselves do not see as compelling truth. The key word here is "argue." That which merely asserts without evidential, logical, and reasoned argument is the kind of popular literature Brother Tasker disliked.

His background and scholarly disposition inclined him toward books that were scholarly, books that were classics in their field—or at least had the potential for being so. He certainly read the classics in missions and, on occasion, recommended them to others. J.W. Phelps, then Secretary-Treasurer of the Missionary Board, wrote to F.G. Smith in November, 1913, saying,

> I must not fail to tell you of an excellent new book that we have recently added to our missionary library—*Missionary Methods, St. Paul's or Ours*. It was recommended by Bro. Tasker. Although you will doubtless not agree with all that the author says, yet his writing is very instructive. Every missionary and every minister of the Church of God should read it. The book can be had at this office for $1.50.

This book certainly did become a classic in the field of missions literature. In an age of colonialism and colonial missions, it was quite revolutionary in its views on missionary methods. Its author, Roland Allen, was an Anglican (Church of England) missionary and the kind of scholarly writer who would have appealed to Brother Tasker. It is interesting indeed that Brother Phelps thought every minister and missionary in the movement should read it–even though they wouldn't likely agree with a lot the author had to say. Since the Church of God at large has never really been that much of a reading church, it is not very likely that ever happened.

One could wonder at this point if the Church of God in India might have fared better if even all of the Missionary Board members had read it and taken it seriously. But it is not likely that happened either. Brother Tasker apparently did and would already have been laboring in India in 1913. How he could have afforded books on his missionary allowance is a mystery–unless he fasted for several days. But, since the book was published in New York in 1912, perhaps he managed to get a copy before sailing for India. What it suggests, among other things, is that somehow he managed to keep abreast of significant publications in the field of missions and other fields.

### Books and More Books

Few missionaries, particularly in those days, had the luxury of collecting a great many books. Their financial means were far too limited and their living conditions much too uncertain for that. Most of them could not, as I once heard Dale Oldham say, "wear the old coat and buy a new book." The old coats they had, probably in abundance, but the new books were either not to be found in the remote corners of the world in which they served or often afforded. Somehow, Brother Tasker managed to buy new books–although not as some of us do today–and move them about from place to place, ending up in Penticton, British Columbia with a good many of them.

I remember being deeply impressed by what I per-ceived to be the sheer size of that library. I realize now it probably wasn't really that big–after all, books and libraries have been part of my professional concern for the past 45 years–but to a farm boy worshiping in a largely rural congregation at that point in my life it was truly impressive. I had always had an intuitive love of books, but had been largely economically and culturally deprived of their riches and pleasure.

Brother Tasker, however, did not just have books, he read them thoroughly and carefully, underlining, making notations in the margins, writing comments and criticisms, in some cases in every available bit of white space. If not enough space was available in the book, he would often glue in extra blank pages to fill with his distinctive handwriting–in ink (with an old-fashioned fountain pen). Perhaps that's where I learned to do much the same— except for the fountain pen and the ink.

On occasion, whenever and wherever possible, he corresponded with writers of books and articles. As Mona Moors Tasker said, "he was always the teacher" and here was no exception. Where he thought a writer had misread a biblical text or failed to take into account some historical or biblical fact, he did not hesitate to point that out in reasoned and detailed argument, sometimes going on for several pages. The letters I have read are kindly and courteous and seem to exude a sense of collegiality. And they do evidence how widely read he was in the Christian literature of his day.

But on occasion, he would, as gently as possible, rebuke a writer or speaker for some statement or other which he found especially unfortunate or objectionable. In a letter written from Bangalore, India on February 21, 1935 to a Reverend T.R. Phillips in Baltimore, Maryland, Brother Tasker expresses his oneness in Christ with Phillips, which he finds "glorious!" But he goes on, in a lengthy paragraph, to entreat Phillips to refrain from using language which he thought unacceptable.

But what occasioned my writing to you in the first place and what in conclusion I earnestly entreat of you now, is never again to publicly label as of Satanic origin the teaching of Christian men as earnest and sincere and spiritual as yourself who feel they have abundant Scriptural warrant and are definitely led of the Spirit in holding eschatological views quite different than your own. Is it not more courteous and more consistent for us fallible men, in such a matter as this where equally good men have always differed, to say we think one another mistaken, than to attribute our opponent's view to the devil? To err may indeed be Satanic, but it is ALSO human—we being what we are. Therefore, so long as man is finite, I hardly think we need to label ALL his mistakes in understanding and teaching as "false doctrine" or attribute them all necessarily to Satan. Our own fallibility is sufficient reason for mistakes and misunderstandings in such points, without drawing the devil into them, which cannot but be offensive to the Christian heart and mind. This is my whole point of contention with you. God bless you and use you more and more.

Here Tasker the thinker and teacher is evident, as well as Tasker the Christian brother. If he believed someone to be in error, he strove as gently as possible to set him or her right. It may be, however, that in his earlier years he was not so kindly or temperate in demeanor or language—and it may be this that put him at odds with the powerbrokers of the Church of God as much as what he had to say (although I can find no indication of that).

### Writing and More Writing

Nowhere is Brother Tasker's scholarly bent more in evidence than in his writing. He was an inveterate letter writer, whether in North America, India, or Syria. Many of these letters are extended scholarly arguments concerning matters of biblical exegesis or doctrine. But not always. One of his extant letters is addressed to a "Mr. Ramsbotham" and consists of a long (nearly four closely-typed pages with narrow margins) and quite learned discussion of the theory of evolution. In his argument against evolution, he cites a number of scientific works on the subject, both for and against, suggesting that he was well-read in this field as well. He knew what the major weakness in the theory were.

A Bishop of the Methodist Church in Southern Asia,

S.K. Mondol, in commending Brother Tasker, says, "Brother Tasker [so he was known even in India] is a keen student of the Bible, a prolific writer whose writings command the attention of the reading public, and is evangelical in his preaching." Indeed he was "a prolific writer," with many, many articles, pamphlets, and books to his credit–to say nothing of what must have been hundreds of letters.

Brother Tasker began his writing for the *Gospel Trumpet* early on. The first of his more than 150 articles in the Trumpet appeared in January, 1901, not many months after his appearance in Moundsville. By 1904, he was a regular writer on biblical and doctrinal subjects, including how to study the Bible. He wrote a number of series of articles, the first of them in 1904-1905, "Christ's Atonement and Its Effects vs. Adam's Sin and Its Effects." This series began on November 24, 1904 and appeared every week except four  through May 11, 1905. If my arithmetic is correct (not a foregone conclusion), that amounts to 21 articles.

Shortly after that series ended, he began on another. "Christian Liberty and Divine Guidance" first appeared  in August, 1905 and ran until December. In effect, that amounted to two books in one year. Whatever Brother Tasker had to say about something, he had a lot to say about it. His thinking and writing skills were considerable and his mind unusually fertile.

Of course, like many of us, he later changed his earliest positions considerably. Scholarly people, thinking people, do. Not many of us would want to be held accountable for all the "eternal truths" we preached and wrote early in our careers. At least, I don't–and neither did he. As one of my former missionary colleagues and good friend, Retha Shultz, so frequently says, "That was then; this is now." Of course, a lot of continuity can be seen between the younger Brother Tasker and the older Brother Tasker, but scholarly people are people who continually grow in knowledge and understanding. He was no exception.

In addition to his "prolific writing" for the *Gospel Trumpet*, Brother Tasker also wrote prolifically for the short-lived *Missionary Herald*, published by the Gospel

Trumpet Company from January, 1910 to February, 1913, "in the interests of missionary work." Of course, he was the Assistant Editor, had spent nearly two years in Egypt, Syria, and India by this time, and was a known and skilled writer, so articles by him would have added pizzaz to any Church of God publication. Generally, one could say, if he wrote it, it was bound to be published. It was not that others were so bad; only that he was that good.

After the "Painful Separation" from the Missionary Board in 1924, virtually all of Brother Tasker's writings were published, generally privately, in India. A number that we do have were printed in Bangalore, South India, by a mission press–possibly Methodist. But he was occasionally published in independent evangelical journals in North America and elsewhere. Much of that writing was done after his retirement in Canada. A "prolific writer whose writings command the attention of the reading public" indeed. Bishop Mondol put it well.

## Missionary

No matter how much we might say about what Brother Tasker was–or who he was, as the case may be–we will quite quickly have to come to what he was above all: a missionary. Thirty four years of his adult life were spent in this calling–thirty six, if we include his nearly two-year missionary tour of Egypt, Syria, and India, 1907-1909. It was this calling that ultimately defined him and provided a much broader context for all his spiritual and scholarly ventures, changing him in irrevocable ways.

Make no mistake about it. Deep, prolonged involvement in other cultures and languages changes us. Such involvement in the personal lives of cultural others, the forming of strong ties of friendship and caring, changes us–that is, if we are open to diversity and change. Life no longer appears in terms of the stark polar opposites Western society has generally taught us from our early childhood. The absolutes of our own inherited cultural existence are often shown to be tendentious, imperfect, incomplete.

Thus, over the course of his later adult life, India changed Brother Tasker, as inexorably as water, in time, changes the shape of the rocks over which it runs. His deep friendship with John A. D. Khan–"the apostle of love," as he was often called in India–about which we will say more presently, changed him. It is a poor missionary indeed who is not thus transformed into a more open, more tolerant, more flexible person, deeply enriched and enriching others. In this, as in other things, Brother Tasker was exceptional.

### Missionary Call

Before going further with this, turn aside with me to Brother Tasker's "call" to missionary life and service. Here again we turn to his article, "How I Became a Foreign Missionary" (*Gospel Trumpet*, November 17, 1921).

From my earliest childhood, missionary influences had been thrown about me. A mother's fervent prayers . . .; the early training of the Sunday-school and home, teaching me to lay aside my pennies in the little missionary box . . .; [and] the frequent entertainment at our house of theological students preparing for the foreign field. All these things sowed the seed, which in due time sprang up when favorable conditions were created by my conversion . . . . Among the missionary spirits of my school and college days, whose addresses, on the occasions of their visits to our city, I remember having listened to with rapt attention, were Pandita Ramabai and Narayan Sheshastri of India, Paton of the New Hebrides, and MacKay of Formosa. . . . The whole outlying Christian world always had my interest and the larger part of my offerings, but somehow India of all fields seemed to be the one ever uppermost in my mind; and as the busy years of preparation passed by . . . the conviction grew that Hindustan would yet be my field of labor.

However, Brother Tasker's almost-a-year-long missionary tour of India a number of years later was not an altogether happy one. He was seriously ill for several weeks and had to cut the trip short and return to America. So when his earlier interest in India powerfully resurfaced some years later while he was teaching at the New York Missionary Home, it was not an altogether welcome intrusion. This time he knew exactly what he was letting himself in for. He continues his story.

Obliged to return to America, I almost concluded that it was the will of God for me to remain there and work at home for the cause of foreign missions. But the vision of the needs of the fields I had visited never left me, and my heart continually turned to the brethren of those lands. My mind and my prayers constantly reverted to them. Indeed, I felt that life had been given back to me only that I might spend it for their sakes. Almost three years passed by. Meanwhile, I had married Minnie B. Criswell, one like-minded with myself, and we often talked together of the foreign work. She fully knew my burden and so was not surprised when I told her one day in New York that India was calling me and that I believed the Lord meant me to return there. [But I hesitated, for the same disease from which the Lord had healed me had carried off Brother Maiden and Sister Jarvis.] And now to return there and take my wife! I really dreaded the place, but the call of duty seemed clear. Somebody must go, and why not I? I simply could not settle down in America. "Go ye," is the command; we ministers of the gospel need to have good reasons for staying at home.

Thus, in 1912, the Taskers embarked for India. Church of God missionary work had begun there in 1897 with the arrival of Gorham G. Tufts. Thaddeus Neff, in *Our Missionaries,* states that in that year at the Grand Junction campmeeting, C.J. Blewitt "initiated the Church of God foreign missionary work by a message he delivered." This, however, is not correct, since Church of God missionary work had begun in Mexico in 1892 with the arrival there of

B.F. Elliott. [2] But by the time the Taskers arrived in India, no fewer than 17 Church of God missionaries had already been on the scene–although only four of them remained in 1912. One of them was Josephine McCrie, a young woman from Ontario, and the movement's first Canadian missionary–at the tender age of 21! She was later to become Brother Tasker's wife, following the death of Sister Minnie Tasker in Bangalore in 1940 (or 1941).

The Missionary Board, in the words of Brother Tasker, its first secretary, was "chosen and appointed by common consent of the ministers present at the annual campmeeting held at Anderson, Ind., June, 1909" (Missionary Board Minutes, 1909). India soon became one of its main concerns. Things were not going well there at all with some of the mission work. D.O. Teasley, Chairman, in his annual report to the Board said: "In India our work is progressing, but not very rapidly in some parts. India still feels the need of directing force. Bro. Tasker's going to India as a permanent missionary will supply a long felt need in this respect" (Minutes, 1912).

This sounds as if the Board expected Brother Tasker to function in some fashion as a kind of field secretary, although that designation was not used until a number of years later. Exactly what Brother Teasley meant by "directing force" is not clear, but the point is that whatever it was, that is what Brother Tasker was to be. Order and direction were needed in the mission work at this point, after more than a decade of autonomous and uncoordinated work—or so the Missionary Board believed. Who better to do it than Brother Tasker? He had been "called" to India (his own words to the Board) and the Board responded by commissioning him to take charge. (I wonder if this might have had some small part to play in his later problems with the Board's Field Secretary?)

[2] Neff gives this date as 1891. Apparently, both John W.V. Smith and Lester A. Crose follow Neff. However, a letter from D.S. Warner to the Gospel Trumpet dated Nov 28, 1892 while he was in Southern California proves quite conclusively that the date of Elliot's embarkation from San Diego to Ensenada, Mexico was in that year, probably early in November.

48

## Work in Lahore and Calcutta

The Taskers began their work in Lahore, in the Punjab, principally in evangelistic and Bible teaching work, remaining there until their first furlough in 1920. Sister Tasker worked among Muslim women, mostly in the zenanas (Hindi, *sanana*), or women's part of the house from which outside males were strictly excluded. It is likely that Brother Tasker traveled a good deal, preaching, teaching, encouraging, and giving support in any way he could to the Indian leaders and workers of the Church of God—those who were the true founders and pioneers of the movement in India: John A. D. Khan; Mosir Moses; P. J. Philip; J. J. M. Roy; R. N. Mundul; and others. Brother Tasker had great respect and appreciation for these persons and developed unusual collegial relationships with them—particularly with John A. D. Khan and J.J.M. Nichols Roy, who appear to have been the hub around which the movement in India rotated. We will have more to say about that presently.

Following their furlough from India in 1920, the Taskers returned in 1921 to settle in Calcutta, much nearer the center of Church of God work. There Sister Tasker continued her zenana work, while Brother Tasker busied himself establishing a small library and large reading room for Indian university students, both Hindu and Muslim. Here is his own description of this venture.

These students, of the 1,200 or so in attendance, whose homes are not in the city itself put up in hostels or immense boarding houses erected especially for them [by the educational authorities]. Here they live, usually several in a room . . . . Strangers in a big city . . . it is evident that their need of suitable places of recreation with a definitely religious atmosphere must be very great. The good Lord . . . sent me a very necessary helper . . . . He is an old friend of our Lahore days, a Bengali and a B.A. He looks after the Reading-room and meets inquirers while I am engaged in another room with my Bible classes [with an eager circle of Hindu and Muslim young men]. My helper, Bro. S.P. Bannerji, also assists me in conducting lantern [slide] lectures on the Life of Christ. . . . You can readily see what an opportunity such a course gives of preaching the gospel in its fullness to hundreds who perhaps have never heard it before. The attendance in our Reading room during November was 598 and in December 688. . . . The attendance appears to be growing. . . . I see many new faces and have many, many conversations upon Christ and Christianity with those who come. . . . The students ask all sorts of questions. I have found them greatly interested in the story of the Passover . . . . So many of the ideas which have been ours from earliest childhood are altogether strange and new to them *(Gospel Trumpet*, March 23, 1923).

In addition to this work, Brother Tasker traveled, spoke in conventions and local congregations, taught Bible classes, even in the Y.M.C.A. and other Christian organizations—later to become a serious problem for him in his relations with the Church of God in America. His collegial and cooperative relations with others extended far beyond the movement, a practice that was to bring him under grave suspicion and censure by the Missionary Board—or at least a few prominent members of it. But that is another story and belongs properly in the next chapter.

Brother Tasker's student work in Calcutta was, of course, conducted in English, since the university and college students there quite likely came from several language backgrounds. More importantly, English had become, under the British Raj (or rule), the language of public education and government business. It was thus natural under the circumstances for much formal public discourse to be conducted in English.

This, perhaps, led to a statement I heard in North America during my early years of research for this book that Brother Tasker was not an "effective" missionary. After all, or so I was told, he had not even learned any Indian language, but did all his preaching and teaching in English and required the assistance of a translator where English was not known. Subsequent research both here and in India indicates that this was not true. According to Mona Moors Tasker, Brother Tasker could preach in both Urdu and Hindi and had at least "conversational ability" in Bengali. A.D. Khan also confirmed that Brother Tasker had learned Urdu "reasonably well."

To be sure, he had not learned Malayalam, the language of much of the church in South India, or Khasi, the language of the church in Meghalaya, Northeast India, but he did not live or work in those areas—apart from occasional visits. Even Indian leaders had to turn to English and the use of translators in such circumstances. Perhaps the accusation of ineffectiveness arose simply from ignorance of the Indian context.

But—just perhaps—it arose from the lack of good public information and the general suspicion of Brother Tasker which certainly existed in official circles of the Church of God at that time. This seems to have led to a general silence about this man—apart from the mention of his name or a few sentences or a paragraph or two—that is certainly not warranted by the records we do have. In this climate, misinformed and, consequently, unreasonable statements can all too easily be made. This long silence has now happily been broken by Church of God writers such as Merle Strege and Barry Callen.

No, by all counts—except one, obviously—Brother Tasker was a highly effective missionary. It was his calling, his passion. And he certainly had the gifts and temperament for it, to say nothing of the spiritual commitment, enthusiasm, and drive. Those in eastern India and Meghalaya who had known Brother Tasker and who were still alive when I first visited India in 1980 spoke of him with great respect and affection.

None more so than A. D. Khan, the son of John A. D. Khan. In his view, it was his father and Brother Tasker who provided the "directing force" for the movement in India. Brother Khan died of pneumonia at age 42 on October 8,

1922, "on my 50th birthday," as Brother Tasker writes on the back of a photograph of Brother Khan in my possession. Less than two years later, Brother Tasker was dismissed by the Missionary Board.

The loss of both men to the Church of God in India in such a short span dealt it a severe blow, a blow from which the Khan family, at least, never recovered. A. D. Khan said, "It was a great pity that when a man of [Brother Tasker's] stature was most needed in this country, his services were lost to the Church of God through the wisdom of men. It would not be extravagant to say that [his] alienation from the movement took away much of its vigor in India, whatever a later generation may aver to the contrary" (from a personal letter to me).   Great pity, indeed!

### Tasker and Khan

It seems appropriate at this point to circle back and pick up the story of the relationship between Brother Tasker and John A.D. Khan. It speaks volumes, in my view, of the kind of man Brother Tasker was and the kind of missionary he became. So much has been written about Brother Khan that it seems a waste of time and paper to say more here. But I'm aware that some readers, at least, may not have read anything about him at all. Those of us in literary circles often assume more than we should–particularly if the circles are quite small.

When Brother Tasker returned to Anderson, Indiana, from his extended missionary tour in 1909, he was accompanied by John ala u' Din Khan, a convert from Islam. This was not Brother Khan's first visit to the United States as a guest of the Church of God. He had come first in 1903, remaining for several months. During that time, he wrote a book, *India's Millions*, published by the Gospel Trumpet Company.[3] He was one of the speakers at the

---

[3] From Gordon Schieck, former missionary to South India and a friend and host of A.D. Khan, the son, who was visiting Canada and the United States, we learned that Brother Khan's family

Peepabun, Ontario campmeeting that year.

Brother Khan had first learned about the Church of God "movement" when he was a university student in Calcutta and responded to a newspaper ad offering, for a small fee, samples of holiness papers published in the United States. Included in the papers sent to Brother Khan was a Gospel Trumpet Company catalogue. The rest you can guess. Of course, he sent for some books, was convinced, and aligned himself with the "movement." He had been a Baptist since his conversion, but had already "come out" and was looking for a place to be at home among a people who felt as he did about denominationalism.

So, when Brother Tasker arrived in India in 1912, he had enjoyed an association and friendship of several years with Brother Khan. Both were university men, and possessed outstanding scholarly ability, which, perhaps, made them natural allies. But they were also kindred spirits in many other ways. A. D. Khan says, "[Brother Tasker] was a frequent visitor in our home. We children were . . . fond of him. In the decade prior to 1922 my father and he were close associates in their evangelical endeavor and I doubt if apart from the Nichols Roys my father had a more intimate friend than G. P. T."

Tasker and Khan were indeed brothers in Christ–and that if you please in colonial India and in an era when Western missionaries generally did not associate too freely or closely with "the natives." Brother Tasker had no patience with imperialist ideology. Besides, in his view, Brother Khan was clearly intellectually and spiritually superior to very many of the Western missionaries of the period. Western culture was Western culture and possessed no innate superiority; good and bad exist in all cultures. All contain much that is noble. And none is free of the taint of human sinfulness.

Brother Khan's unexpected death was a great blow to

---

had never seen this book, although they knew of it. So, through the kindness of Richard Snyder, Director of Library Services at Anderson University, we saw to it that Brother Khan's son returned to India bearing a copy of it.

Brother Tasker–as it was to the whole movement in India. The church had lost a prophet, an "apostle of love," but he had lost a great deal more. He had learned much about India and the Indian "mind" (whatever that is, apart from being an anthropologically unhelpful term), as well as about theology and mission, from his Indian brother. Never again would he have a friend, colleague and confidante of that caliber–although Brother Nichols Roy came close. Brother Khan was irreplaceable.

Many times in his final years, I heard Brother Tasker lament the death of Brother Khan, a death which he believed was not brought about by pneumonia as such, but by "a broken heart." Instead of fighting his illness, he simply gave up. Whether or not that is the case, we have no way of knowing. But Brother Tasker believed it to be so. And, since the "broken heart" had to do with the arrival in India of Floyd Heinly and his perceived role as the watchdog of the Anderson brethren and the hardening attitude of the Missionary Board to Indian independence, with its concomitant loss of "freedom of the Spirit" within the movement in India, it doubtless affected Brother Tasker's relationship with the Board.

Within a year of Brother Khan's death, the pot began to boil and before another year had ended, had boiled over, putting to an end a missionary career within the Church of God that might indeed have resulted in a much larger Church of God community in eastern India today. That is not given to us to know. But A.D. Khan firmly believed it. And so do others of us. However, it was not believed at the time by the majority of the Missionary Board members and a few other powerful persons. In the end, that's all that mattered.

### Finally

And so to the question, what went wrong when everything went wrong? Why did the Missionary Board feel it necessary to reprimand Brother Tasker and why was he unwilling—at least in the officially published view—to accept their attempts to discipline and control him, thus leading to his "excommunication," as A. D. Khan put it? These are no easy questions to answer. They weren't then and they certainly are not now. Even so, if we are to "set the record straight" (A.D. Khan's words), we must make the attempt.

It is not at all easy to be even-handed from this point on in the telling of the story. What happened was, in my view, a tragedy—probably for everyone involved. It would be easy to fly to Brother Tasker's defense, lamenting the rather extreme sectarianism and short-sightedness with which he was treated. But that would be not altogether fair. Following A.D. Khan's fine example, we must recognize that such a response is much too simplistic and self-serving. And, above all, it is probably historical hindsight, which is itself basically unfair.

## Chapter 3

## WHAT WENT WRONG
## WHEN EVERYTHING WENT WRONG?

On June 11, 1924, the Resolutions Committee of the Missionary Board brought a multi-part resolution to the Board concerning Brother Tasker. After lengthy discussion, it was adopted by a vote of twelve to one (two board members were absent). The resolution reads as follows:

WHEREAS a mass of correspondence between our Secretary and Bro. G. P. Tasker reveals the fact that Brother Tasker has grown out of sympathy with the work which this Board seeks to do in India; and

WHEREAS very numerous complaints have come to us from influential brethren in this and foreign lands vigorously protesting against our supporting a man whom they believe to be working at cross purposes with the vast majority of the brethren in the home land;

Therefore, be it RESOLVED: That this Board sever its relations with Bro. G. P. Tasker and wife at once; and that both he and the Field Secretary of India be notified at once to this effect; and

RESOLVED that we instruct the Field Secretary of India to look after and provide for the temporary support of the Taskers until such a time in the near future when the Board can honorably be relieved of their support, such term not to extend beyond

Jan.1, 1925. The Field Secretary of India will take the necessary steps as soon as possible to close up or otherwise arrange for the work in Calcutta formerly under Brother Tasker's care, and

Be it further RESOLVED that we would not by this action cast any reflection upon Brother Tasker's moral character. We have known him for many years as a gentleman of high moral character and still regard him as such. In like manner we esteem his wife to be a lady of the highest moral character.

It is with feelings of deep sorrow that we terminate the relations of many years, but we do so driven by the convictions of our consciences that in our trustee capacity it is our duty to support missionaries on the foreign field who are able conscientiously to teach in harmony with and work for the accomplishment of the purposes sought by the people whose gifts we administer.

### The Resolution

This resolution seems to make it quite clear how the Missionary Board viewed the situation. First, Brother Tasker had "grown out of sympathy with the work the Board seeks to do in India." Second, the "numerous complaints" from "brethren" both in America and overseas, "protesting our supporting a man whom they believe to be working at cross purposes with the vast majority of the brethren in the home land." These, in the main, are the charges.

At first glance, these charges seem overly-general and ambiguous. "Out of sympathy?" "Working at cross pur-poses?" One can't help but think that something much deeper and more personal lies behind them. The Board made it quite clear in the resolution and their discussion of it that Brother Tasker had not committed any moral or legal offense, nor had he lost his commitment to Christ or his zeal for missions "to the heathen" (that unfortunate term used in those days—even by Brother Tasker). In India, he was generally well liked and respected. Former missionaries and Indian Christians with whom I spoke were quite clear about that.

What, then, was the Missionary Board seeking to do in India with which Brother Tasker had grown "out of sympathy?" That certainly could not have been a trivial matter. He had shown himself much too broad-minded to have been concerned about a minor difference of opinion. One leading Board member, at least, considered him to be "dangerously liberal," a view probably shared by most other members as well. But that label helps us not at all to understand what was going on. Generally, "liberal" is used to label someone who is to our left theologically or ideologically and whose views threaten our own.

## Missionary Board Presence in India

The important question here, as I see it, is what the Board perceived itself as trying to do in India. Generally, of course, the purpose of the Board—and doubtless those supporting them—was to win Indians to Christ. That was also Brother Tasker's concern, in fact, his main concern. But, more specifically, the Board was concerned to raise up Church of God congregations, congregations that would grow and eventually become self-supporting. Brother Tasker was certainly not "out of sympathy" with that, although he did not see it as absolutely essential in every case. What was more important was bringing Indians to Christ.

Nevertheless, he was generally committed to the idea of planting Church of God congregations. During the Tasker's furlough from India in 1920-1921, Brother Tasker proposed to the Board that "district work" be opened up in India. His concern was those hundreds of districts where no churches, Indian workers, or missionaries of any kind were to be found. The work in the city of Lahore had been institutional work in the main and was in the process of closing down. He wanted to get out among the common people and preach Christ where he had not been preached. If we do not do this, he said, we really have no place in India. His passion for preaching the gospel among the masses of India was very deep. This, as Sister Nichols Roy said, he pleaded "in tears."

When asked by the Board in session what opening up a district work would cost, he told them it would require "about $10,000" just to get started. In 1921, this was a small fortune and probably well beyond the means of the Board–especially when the total budget for India was less than $44,000–and very difficult to raise, as it was. In addition, requests for major budget increases and special funds were coming in from every field. The Board must have felt they were expected to get blood out of a turnip.

So, as one would expect, the Board, while readily admitting that Brother Tasker was probably correct in his assessment and concern, had to turn down his proposal. A pity, then, that some members did not remember this in the heat of the events of 1924, when he was charged with having spent eight years in Lahore "for nothing" and at significant cost to the Board. And further, that his work in Calcutta was not yielding any "returns" for the Church of God–precisely what he had told the Board three years earlier. But, when trying to get out of a seemingly intolerable situation, one does tend to grasp at straws– even imaginary ones.

And the Missionary Board was in a most difficult situation. Some members agonized over the problem. Brother Tasker was their friend and colleague, a man for whom they had respect and affection. How could this have happened? What had gone wrong? However, a few members–including, unfortunately, the most powerful ones –had few qualms about disfellowshipping someone whom they saw as having come to disagree with the doctrine they believed to be the truth of the Gospel. Besides, given Brother Tasker's stature in the movement, his "dangerous liberalism" could not help but reflect on the Board and possibly lead to some disaffection and loss of support.

## Essential Reformation Truths

All of this furor would not have been caused by the fact that some–and not likely a majority–thought Brother Tasker an unsuccessful missionary. Thus, what the

Missionary Board saw itself as "trying to do in India" had to go well beyond winning Indians to Christ and gathering them into self-sustaining congregations of the Church of God–whether or not they saw him as doing that successfully.

No, Brother Tasker's failure was the failure to take a firm stand for what most of the Board saw as essential "reformation truths": that the shining forth of the evening light and the emergence of the church of God movement as the singular bearer of that light was prophesied in Scripture; and, that sect Babylon was under the judgment of God and to be "threshed" and sifted for souls whose hearts were pure toward God.

In other words, missionary work was not just the proclamation of Christ to non-Christians, but the proclamation of the evening light in the so-called Christian communities of sect Babylon, in an attempt to persuade "precious souls" to come out of her into the fellowship of the saints in the evening light. Not only was Brother Tasker not doing that, he was quite vocal about not doing it and his practical and biblical reasons for not doing it.

Even worse, he was cooperating fully with sect Babylon and even benefiting them by his preaching and teaching. After all, had he not wanted to go into "district work" in some area where no other mission or church was working, so that he would not be "in competition" with them? Trying to win them over was precisely what he was expected by the "influential brethren" in America to be doing.

The Resolution was, then, deliberately ambiguous. The real theological concerns of Board members and others vocally critical of Brother Tasker were, in effect, passed over in the Resolution–which, of course, gives the impression that the real concerns (or, if you like, the primary concerns) of the Board were neither theological, moral, nor spiritual. The Board's instructions to the Resolutions Committee makes this quite clear:

The Resolutions Committee was instructed to draw up a resolution that should have nothing to say about the theological questions involved in Brother Tasker's work on the mission field, but merely dealing with the business relationship of Brother Tasker and the Board as representatives of the church and with Tasker as representative of the Board and the church, the resolution to include the willingness of the Board to return Brother Tasker to America if he wishes to come and to make arrangements for his support for a certain length of time until final arrangements for his work and his return to America could be completed (Minutes, June 10, 1924).

From the Missionary Board's perspective, Brother Tasker was, indeed, both "out of sympathy" with what they were trying to do in India and, as well, working "at cross purposes with the vast majority of the brethren in the homeland." That he did not agree with what they were trying to do was beside the point, as far as they were concerned. As long as he was being sent and supported by the Board, he should either "fall into line" or find some other group to work with.

Instead, he was trying to convert others to his point of view, so one Board member lamented. He does not have a "clear vision of the church of God," and "does not believe the doctrines of this movement," another member added. If he is allowed to remain in India, he will "poison the native leaders" and "the work will be lost to us," said a third (Missionary Board Minutes).

It may well be that given the circumstances and the commitment of the Board and their supporters to the "come-out" doctrine, they had little choice but to dismiss the Taskers. Some pastors and laypersons were upset by what they believed Brother Tasker was saying and doing. He had traveled extensively while in the United States on furlough, speaking in a variety of settings. And he was not one to proclaim only what people wanted to hear—or necessarily to proclaim it at all. Not only must the Gospel be preached, but it must be preached in the language and metaphors with which they were familiar. Nothing else was the Gospel.

Brother Tasker, however, openly proclaimed what he believed the Spirit of God had led him to in the Scriptures and what he had learned from his experience in India. This was, by and large, unfamiliar in Church of God congregations. That some of his hearers would dislike it and write to the Missionary Board about their dislike was a foregone conclusion–particularly if they knew Board members were, in a sense, "eager" to hear about such things. Therefore, as the Resolution has it, "very numerous complaints" possibly did come into the Board office–some, at any rate, although "very numerous" does have a good rhetorical effect. It is not easy to see what "influential brethren" they came from "in foreign lands," however. The "influential brethren" in India were generally in support of Brother Tasker and his views. The only "influential" person related to the work there who would have complained quite loudly and at length to the Board was the Field Secretary for India–and that was his job. Some new missionaries were also probably sympathetic with the Board's viewpoint, but could hardly be called "influential brethren."

Other "influential brethren in foreign lands" knew only what they were told by "influential brethren" in this land. And why the Board would have worried much about those complaints anyway is difficult to see. After all, they were not even potential contributors to the Board's budget. But, "influential brethren in foreign lands" seems to lend greater weight to the Resolution. So, although general and vague, it served the purpose well.

### Budget Concerns

The budget! Ah, now we come to an underlying issue. Brother Tasker himself believed that the whole thing had to do with budget problems and worries. In the case of a letter from Ontario demanding that the Board not send Josephine McCrie back to India after her furlough because she claimed "the tongues experience," the Executive Committee of the Board came vigorously to her defense. She did not practice this in public, the upset pastor was told, but used it only as a private prayer language in accordance with the Scriptures. And she was duly sent back to India with the Board's full blessing and support.

You see? No budget support from Canada to worry

about–at least, no major budget support. Had there been, Sister McCrie would likely have been dealt with differently. This was not lost on Brother Tasker. He overlooked, however, that "tongues" (as opposed to pentecostalism) was not a critical issue with the Board, especially F.G. Smith, who fully accepted the validity of tongues as a prayer language. The "come out" doctrine was quite another matter. No one could be ambivalent or in opposition on that question and expect any tolerance at all from the powers-that-were.

However, our sympathies are also with the Board in this case. Trying to raise a missions budget in a fellowship of congregations not all that enthused, as a whole, about "missions to the heathen" in the first place, was a truly daunting task. Many pastors and elders of churches had major problems themselves just keeping the church doors open and food on their tables. It was easy then—as it is now—under the circumstances, for vision to be focused on the local parish (as in "out of sight, out of mind").

In 1924, the Church of God in the United States of America consisted of about 650 congregations (according to the 1924 Yearbook of the Church of God), and most of them very small (average size about 40 adherents, with only 45 of them being 100 members or more). The total number of adherents was just over 25,000. This is a very small pool from which to raise a total Missionary Board budget of $144,000–which, in the 1923-24 budget year, fell $26,000 short, leaving them only $118,000. A major problem, no doubt about it. It seems they hadn't yet learned about deficit spending.

Any missionary who was seen as "not being in line with this movement" or who did not have "a clear vision of the church of God," could potentially cause the trickle of funds from local churches to slow considerably, or dry up altogether. In addition to challenging and offending the doctrinal sensibilities of the elders of the movement, Brother Tasker was endangering the very life blood of the Missionary Board. Their budget woes were very real and burdensome and not to be taken lightly.

The President of the Board stated that not so much Brother Tasker's public preaching, but his private conversations had spread his views everywhere in the Church and was causing "the withholding of funds." The Board simply did not know "how to stay off the tide of opposition to Brother Tasker in this country any longer." [3] Even though this is probably a dramatic over-statement made for its rhetorical effect–after all, "a tide of opposition everywhere " suggests a Church-wide concern–believe me when I say this is no light matter. Servants of the Church, such as J.W. Phelps, the Secretary-Treasurer of the Missionary Board during this period, struggled almost desperately at times to meet financial obligations related to the mission work overseas. One cannot but be sympathetic. The fear of offending donors or potential donors–or of some indiscrete, overly-frank missionary doing so–is very real. Undoubtedly it has tilted the balances in many a policy decision.

Brother Tasker did not think it should, but, then, he was not left to try to find the needed dollars elsewhere, was he? More sympathy on his part in this matter might have given some Board members pause. But then, it might not have either, particularly those who were much less concerned about the budget than about defending what they saw as the purity of the "gospel" committed by God to "this reformation movement."

The rest of the Missionary Board's conversation around this Resolution is of little consequence–or substance, in some cases, as with the unfounded comment by a senior member that "there was constant friction" between Brother

---

[3] Additional information has just come from David Davis. In Minnie Tasker's Bible, which came to him indirectly from Mona Moors Tasker, Brother Tasker has written an outline chronology in abbreviated form of his missionary career. Many of the entries reveal new information, but usually without comment. This one, then, stands out: "Sailed New York July 1921 for Liverpool. Urged by Smith and Reardon as Ohio ministers were agitating against me." Some from other states may well have joined in the "agitation," but Brother Smith may also have exaggerated the scope of the opposition for rhetorical effect. This is not to minimize the seriousness of the problem, but only to counter the notion that opposition to Brother Tasker was "widespread"—a virtual "tide" about to engulf the Anderson brethren.

Tasker and his fellow missionaries. (I say unfounded because missionaries who were there deny that this was the case and in Missionary Board correspondence and Minutes I could find no mention of this.) No mention, that is, except of Brother Tasker's relations with the newly appointed India Secretary of the Missionary Board, a subject we must surely look into at some length, since it may have set off much of the later furor.

Brother Tasker may well have questioned the come-outer enthusiasm of one or two of the newly appointed missionaries, but he was normally a kind and gracious man, even when dealing with what he saw as individual ignorance and dogmatism.[4] "Friction," however, is probably too strong a term—except in the case of "poor" Brother Heinly, as Brother Tasker later referred to him (not with pity or condescension, but with genuine sympathy for a fellow missionary caught between a rock and hard place, thanks to the short-sightedness of others).

We must, in the meantime, remember that Board members, with the exception of Brother F.G. Smith, who had spent two years in Syria and Brother Riggle, who had spent a year, also in Syria (now Lebanon), were generally not themselves former missionaries and apart from a quick visit here or there by a few of them had little practical basis for understanding the written and verbal reports given them. Misunderstandings and misinterpretations were bound to occur—and often did—due largely to an unavoidable ignorance of the context of the information from the field. Not infrequently, conclusions were reached on the basis of skimpy evidence or a misunderstanding of what evidence they had.

Further, a few, at least, of the Board's sources of information must be doubted. Some of the complaints in the Board meeting by Board members do indeed sound more like rumors than anything else. The important point,

---

[4] I use the word "normally" here advisedly. The controversy with the Missionary Board and the leaders of the Gospel Trumpet Company was, to say the least, a very abnormal and unusually trying set of circumstances. Even calm tempers could become heated—and apparently did so to everyone's loss.

however, is that whether correct or incorrect, rumor or fact, the perception of most was that Brother Tasker deserved to be dismissed, and so he was.

## Evalyn Nichols Roy

The day after the Resolution was actually approved by the Board, Evalyn Nichols Roy arrived in Anderson from India. The Missionary Board Minutes state: "Sister Roy, who had now arrived in Anderson, was called in that the Board might have her views in regard to whether or not Brother Tasker and wife should be called home from India" (June 12, 1924). One wonders if the Board was still undecided at that point and was willing to be persuaded otherwise. If Sister Nichols Roy had been powerful in her defense of the Taskers, would the Board have rescinded its earlier decision? Not likely, as the conversation with Sister Nichols Roy makes clear. Why then the Secretary's wording of the record: "whether or not Brother Tasker and wife should be called home from India?"

It may be that both the Board and individual members of the Missionary Board had already been sounding out missionaries and Indian church leaders—as well as "influential brethren" concerning their personal views of Brother Tasker. C. J. Blewitt, the Board's agent in New York, seems from correspondence with the Board to have been quite insistent, long before the meeting in which a resolution of dismissal was discussed, that Brother Tasker must be "recalled" at the earliest possible moment. In the Board meeting later, he reported to the Board that "Brother and Sister Roy think that Brother Tasker is ahead of the rest of the church in his thinking . . ." (Minutes, June 10, 1924). So he may indeed have been gathering "evidence" to support his call for dismissal.

E.E. Byrum, in the same session, speaks of "much damaging evidence against Brother Tasker" and "the strong ultimatum that had been given him fully nine months before." Since he had been given ample opportunity "to find his way out and had not done so," it must be that he was waiting for the Board to do it for him. That would have been in 1923. We can, I think, reasonably infer from all of this that much correspondence was exchanged between Board members and others and opinions solicited.

Sister Nichols Roy, however, vigorously defended Brother Tasker in the Board meeting and told them that he was the only "evangelist" the church in northern India now had. Brother Heinly, she said, is "a fine business man and a good preacher," but he is in no way the caliber of Brother Tasker. Her reasons for not "calling Brother Tasker home from India" (which, I think, is simply a euphemistic way of saying "fire him") are well worth noting:

1. That Brother Tasker was at last settled in the work in India and that he was doing well that which no one else can do.

2. That although Brother Tasker has talked too much as her husband had already told him, yet he had not meant so much by his talk as the Board had supposed. His heart was right, although he had seemingly criticized very severely.

3. That although Tasker had gone too far in his criticism, yet he felt there was really something wrong with the church and that he was seeking as best he could to correct it.

4. That there were already too few missionaries in India, and to withdraw one of the oldest and ablest would be a terrible blow to the work now, and so discourage the natives who would scarcely be able to stand such a move on the part of the Board.

5. That to recall Tasker now from the field without giving the Indian church a chance to have choice in the matter was not fair to the Indian church. [An argument that would have left the Board not only unmoved, but perhaps incredulous. What a strange and "liberal" notion! What had the Indian church to do with this matter?]

We can only guess at what Sister Nichols Roy might have thought or said had she known her interview was quite likely only a formality, possibly designed to appease missionary opinion in India and that the case had been formally decided the day before. As soon as her "interview" was over, the Board appears simply to have gone about other business as though Sister Nichols Roy had not even appeared—at least as far as the record is concerned.

It is possible, in fact, to conclude–and Brother Tasker, among others, certainly did so–that the case had been settled in the minds of the most powerful Board members long before it came "to trial." Nothing the few undecided members, or Sister Nichols Roy, could say would make any difference in the outcome. One member protested rather feebly and another voted against the resolution. But, in the view of those who really made the rules–and they were always careful to do that in the shadow of others– Brother Tasker was clearly "not in line with this Movement." Further, he had shown no inclination to "get in line" by changing his views–something one Board member said he had "little hope" would ever happen.

But one must, by all means, give the impression of fair and impartial proceedings. It seems that some members were indeed undecided and reluctant to take action, but not so the powerbrokers. They were, after all, the guardians and keepers of the doctrine Brother Tasker so openly criticized. They were defending what they passionately believed to be God's final revelation to his only true and called-out people. In fairness to them, we must recognize that they sincerely believed they were simply doing their duty to God and "the movement" which God had brought into being–just as Brother Tasker passionately believed he was doing his duty to Christ and to the Church of God in India.

### The India Secretary of the Missionary Board

I do not mean to leave the impression that the Missionary Board had no administrative concerns with Brother Tasker. They most certainly did. He perceived the "movement" solidifying itself into a denomination–the very thing the it was supposed to be fighting–and then in good colonialist fashion imposing the resulting organizational structure on the Church in India. "Man-rule" was being substituted for "Holy Spirit-rule," so Brother Tasker (and others) believed. The freedom of the Spirit was being lost and he would not accept that imposition in India. I quote again from A.D. Khan, the eldest son of Brother Khan:

Indeed I have had the feeling that the Missionary Board, or whatever regimen then held sway, failed to appreciate adequately the fact that in spite of his impatience with dogmatic stance and the rigidity of posture such as seemed to be emerging in the Church of God of the time, the depth of his commitment to Christ and the sincerity of his sense of mission were never in doubt. . . (Personal letter, November 10, 1979).

The statement concerning the "dogmatic stances and the rigidity of posture such as seemed to be emerging in the Church of God [in the United States] of the time" probably well expresses what both Brother Tasker and the leaders of the Church of God in India were seeing. And they were deeply concerned about the direction being taken in Anderson. A.D. Khan speaks of the close association and like-mindedness of his father and Brother Tasker in these and other matters. Both saw the changes in thinking in Anderson as deeply disturbing. He continues:

This meant also a community of interest in concerns relating to their work which were exercising their minds over the line of thinking emerging in Anderson shortly after F.W. Heinly's arrival in Calcutta. I suspect they were missing the freedom of the Spirit that marked the pioneers of the movement, something they felt was basic but was being lost under the new dispensation. It was a natural reaction which, alas, the leadership did not take into account. Young as I was I could sense their uneasiness over the changes they feared would imperil the future of their relationship with the new regime. The clouds were gathering on the horizon. . . . Concurrently for the same reasons leaders in Shillong showed signs of unhappiness, though the Nichols Roys did not move toward an open breach.

## A Remarkable Revolution

What was happening in Anderson? According to John W.V. Smith, "a remarkable organizational revolution" that took place in the twelve years between 1916 and 1928. Here is his own attempt to put it in a nutshell:

In that brief time the tradition of the previous third of a century had been changed. An assembly had been organized, officers were elected, and boards and committees had been established to take care of the church's general corporate responsibilities. Perhaps an even greater transition than the more sophisticated organization itself was the financial system made necessary by the budgets of these developing agencies. The power structure shifted from Holy Spirit leadership with only minimal informal organization to what was hoped to be Holy Spirit leadership with formal organization (*The Quest for Holiness and Unity*, p.223).

What is really remarkable about this "organizational revolution" is that some, at least, of the power brokers of "the-movement-now-becoming-something-else" (as critics saw it) actually seemed to deny that it was happening and continued to reiterate, almost vehemently, the anti-sectarian, anti-denominational ideology of the first generation. Even while apparently taking on denominational trappings, they were condemning "man-rule" and human organization. F.G. Smith, in a booklet written in 1926, made this remarkable statement on the Church of God position on "the church question" (Or was it really his own protest against what he saw as a regrettable turning of the tide?)

We hold sectarianism to be anti-Scriptural, and

claim that sectarianism has resulted from two things in particular: (1) the teaching and practice of unscriptural doctrines, and (2) the substitution of the human for divine in schemes of church organization and government. We regard every effort to organize the church of Christ humanly as being denominational and sectarian ("Brief Sketch of the Origin, Growth, and Distinctive Doctrine of the Church of God Reformation Movement," p.14).

( Permit me an aside here. In my mind's eye, I can see Brother Tasker bouncing about in agitation loudly expressing his great scorn at this statement with the usual exclamation he reserved for such cases: *"Pfah!"* To get the real effect of that, you have to pronounce the p and *f* as one sound, not two–a kind of explosive sound, quite dramatic when executed properly.) [5]

For Brother Tasker, as well as for the leaders of the Church of God in India, it was bad enough to create such a perversion of what they perceived the "movement" to be all about, but to insist on exporting it across the oceans and imposing it on India was galling indeed. And it certainly must have appeared then, as it does now, that Floyd W. Heinly was appointed to India in 1918 for exactly that purpose. Thus, it was almost a foregone conclusion from the very beginning that trouble would result. Contrary to A.D. Khan, clouds were not gathering on the horizon; they had gathered overhead–darkly!

---

[5] In fairness to Brother Smith (as I have suggested above), it needs to be noted that he *may have* been stating this position as his renewed stand against the "organizational revolution" which was going on in Anderson. That revolution had been set in motion before his time by the setting up of the Missionary Board. But in the beginning, at least, he seems to have approved both of it and of the establishment of the Ministerial Assembly. What resulted in the end may not have been to his liking, however, so now he sounds a warning. Perhaps. It is also possible that he was becoming increasingly uneasy with the Ministerial Assembly's growing demand for control of the Church's corporate life. Eventually this led to his own removal from power—something he may have intuitively feared.

*Floyd W. Heinly*

I doubt that the conflict which had developed between Brothers Tasker and Heinly was, as some leading members of the Board intimated, a personality conflict and that Brother Tasker was the troublemaker. In fact, some argued that one of the important (administrative) reasons he should be brought home was because he could not get on with Brother Heinly–or other missionaries for that matter–who was the official "power" of the Board in India. From all I can learn about Brother Heinly at this point, he seems to have been a competent business man and an excellent administrator–but a complete company man–and little more. For a few years, he had served as a "stenographer" to D.O. Teasley in the New York Missionary Home. Then for a few more years, he worked in the sales department of the Gospel Trumpet Company, finally becoming managing editor of the *Gospel Trumpet*, a position he held for six years before his appointment to India as Field Secretary.

From all reports, particularly from India and from former missionaries there, he was a kind, friendly, and gentle man. In time, it appears, he became a fairly good field missionary, initiating valuable work in an area now known as Bangladesh—at least laying the groundwork for what Robert and Frances Clark were later to spend many years building upon.

But at 31 he was much younger and infinitely less experienced than Brother Tasker–or anyone else active on the Indian scene, for that matter–and in no way his intellectual or ministerial equal. His gifts appear to have been organization and administration, which the Board felt were needed to get people "in line," whether missionaries or Indians. The Board worried, however, that Brother Heinly might not be up to the task. This was discussed at some length by the Board in June, 1918:

Information having in some way reached the Board that there was danger of Brother Heinly's taking up with Brother Tasker's views [published earlier in

India in the booklet, *The Church in Its Scriptural Senses*, fear was expressed by different members of the Board      that Brother Heinly was not strong enough [biblically? doctrinally?] to cope with the Indian situation. . . . The opinion was expressed that a good, solid man should accompany Brother Heinly.

So it seems that the Board was concerned to send an official representative–a kind of *de facto* bishop (that is, someone who functioned as a missionary bishop without using that name, or admitting to its validity)–who could deal with Brother Tasker and other Indian leaders who assumed it was they who actually were in charge of the work in India. This would have been a most difficult task for a senior, theologically prepared, and experienced person. To give the task over to one so young, untrained, and inexperienced was nothing short of (very unwise).

It demonstrates, among other things, how very little the Board as a whole actually knew about missions and mission work in India at that point. That it was very unfair to as fine a man as Brother Heinly seems to have been did not—because it probably could not under those circumstances—occur to them. By such action, they were putting him into a volatile, if not impossible, situation. The result was predictably disastrous.

In a subsequent session of the Board, Brother Heinly was specifically asked where he stood in relation to Brother Tasker's book, *The Church in Its Scriptural Senses.* [6] He replied in effect that when he read the book, he was convinced by it and adopted a more "modern view" than that which he had held while at the Gospel Trumpet office. But subsequently, he confessed, a sermon delivered by F.G. Smith brought him around to the "correct" view as held by this reformation, even though he himself could not "prove his belief by prophecy." But he felt

---

[6] This, unfortunately, is one of Brother Tasker's writings that we have not been able to find. It was apparently circulated in North America at one point, but seems now not to be available even in private collections. I hope that we shall yet find it.

that he could, however, prove it by "philosophy" (whatever that was).

That ought to have told the Board right then and there that Brother Heinley was considerably out of his depth at that point in his life. Perhaps it did. But he hurriedly redeemed himself by saying, "not withstanding some mistakes made by this reformation" he still believed it to be "the true and final reformation." Theologically, he seemed to follow whoever got to speak last. In this case, it was Brother Smith.

A Board member then produced "evidence" showing that Brother Nichols Roy was not teaching the reformation doctrine of sanctification. Brother Heinly replied that he "strongly favors" the teaching of sanctification as believed by "this movement." But, again, I wonder if he could defend that view scripturally—or even "by philosophy"—or if Brother Nichols Roy would have had the last word on that subject? After all, Brother Nichols Roy was a university trained man and a noted Bible teacher. Quite likely, his ability to argue matters "by philosophy" was not insignificant either.

However, I do not think Brother Heinly himself was the problem. He made no pretense of being a biblical or theological scholar. Here he was clearly out of his depth and knew it. He was simply a good man given the impossible assignment—for him at that point—of trying to cope with an explosive situation that was every bit as much the Board's making as it was anyone else's. (One can argue that he should have known better than to have taken such a job, given his ministerial inexperence and lack of training. But that's another question.)

The major problem was the office he was sent to fill: "India Secretary of the Missionary Board." Even more specifically, it was the problem of the creation of the office itself in the missionary work of a movement which claimed to eschew all such sectarian and denominational structures. Lester A. Crose puts it well and—as much as anything else, in affection and respect for him and his contribution to the missionary life of the Church of God—I quote him in full:

Following a practice commonly practiced by most Protestant missions, the Missionary Board created the office of field secretary which was held by a missionary at each mission. This person became the representative of the Board. This was initiated when Floyd W. Heinly and his family were sent to India as missionaries *to assume control over our missionary endeavors there.* . . . For a time, the results were almost disastrous in India. In retrospect, we can say that this was a major error committed by the young Board relative to the work in India. Recall for a moment the high quality of able leadership in the Indian church. Strong letters of protest from these leaders were received by the Board. They objected to having a missionary appointed by the Missionary Board in America to manage the work of the Church of God in India. After all, the movement in India had its own missionary board, and the brethren felt they were capable under God to give guidance to the work in their own county. *But this pattern of organization of a mission followed exactly the colonial system of control and administration.* The common saying was, "He who pays the piper calls the tune" (*Passport for a Reformation*, p.52f., italics mine).

### Foreign Authority and Control

This, then, was the nub of the administrative problem in India. Brother Tasker and those with whom he stood most strenuously objected to the imposition of the office of India Secretary and the American authority and control it was seen to represent. They protested in vain. E.E. Byrum, then Vice-President of the Missionary Board, summed up his rule of thumb for dealing with all such insubordination: "threaten to withdraw our funds and they will quickly come to time." Indeed, those who pay the piper are sure they have the inalienable right to call the tune. Or, as I've often said, the Golden Rule of colonial missions is, "Those who have the gold make the rules."

Ultimately, five missionaries, reportedly, including the

Nichols Roys and Josephine McCrie, resigned in protest of this move and the dismissal of the Taskers. (I have not been able to determine who the other two were—perhaps Indians. The record is confused here.) Indeed, the results were "almost disastrous," as Brother Crose put it. On second thought, perhaps we can leave out the "almost." We know from several field sources that this move was a terrible blow to John A.D. Khan. He felt that the principles of the movement had been betrayed and that he was to be collared, leashed, and led about by an inexperienced and largely educationally and apostolically unqualified young American simply because that person was the official representative and spokesperson of the American Missionary Board. Where now the acclaim with which he was met everywhere on his collegial visits to the United States? Why was he now to be controlled and directed from there—"harnassed for this movement?"

As I mentioned earlier, Brother Tasker believed that Brother Khan simply lost heart and, during a bout with influenza and pneumonia, gave up and died. His treatment by the Board had "broken his heart." Brother Tasker writes of this at some length in *An Appeal*.

Sister Nichols Roy stated to the Board that the death of Brother Khan had been a bitter and devastating blow to the movement in India. If you "bring the Taskers home," she had told them, the bottom would drop out of things. At least for a time, it did. With both Brother Khan and Brother Tasker gone, much of the driving power of the Church of God in India was lost. The work continued strongly in Meghalaya because of the Nichols Roys—although eventually independently of the Missionary Board. In South India, the work of the Church of God continued—although less strongly—because of P.J. Philip and his associates, who chose to remain under the formal financial and administrative control of the Missionary Board.

The removal of Brothers Khan and Tasker in Eastern India created a vacuum that simply could not be filled. The ground that was lost could not be regained and much of the work there had to begin again much later. (Robert H. Clark, longtime Church of God Missionary to India has written very concisely and helpfully about this in an unpublished paper in my possession.)

## Summary and Conclusion

By this time, I'm not even quite sure myself what I've said or haven't said. I began by talking about the Missionary Board's Resolution to withdraw, or separate the Tasker's from the work of the Church of God in India. This, I concluded, was based on three major concerns: (1) that Brother Tasker's theology was no longer fully in line with that which the "influential brethren" of the Church of God in the United States believed they held ("no longer" suggests that it once was, which I question, although, to be sure, Brother Tasker did constantly grow and change intellectually and theologically); (2) that Brother Tasker refused, most adamantly and publicly, to accept the novel direction of the Church concerning organization and structure and, in particular, the Missionary Board's insistence that he must submit to the authority and control of the India Secretary of the Missionary Board, as he had tacitly agreed to do in at least tentatively approving the equally novel Missionary Manual, prepared in 1923; and (3) that missions offerings from congregations either were or would be withheld due to the metaphorical "flood" of criticism of Brother Tasker's novel doctrinal and mis-siological views.

In the minds of some senior Board members, the fundamental issue was theological. While Brother Tasker was on furlough, many conversations–mostly private–took place concerning his stance on various questions of "reformation" doctrine. Clearly, what he was expected to do to redeem himself and his missionary career was to repent of his heretical views and promise never again to preach such things. Thus the "stern warning" from the Board spoken about in their correspondence with him following his furlough—as well as warnings from Brother Smith and remonstrances from Brother Reardon during the furlough itself.

But Brother Tasker was not about to surrender his theological mind to what he might today have called "group think." He believed theology must be argued, not dogmatically asserted, particularly with penalties attached for those who did not "fall into line"–that infamous authoritarian phrase that occurs so frequently in Board deliberations of that period. This seemed to him clearly to deny the freedom and leadership of the Spirit in the intellectual life of the Christian community.

It might have occurred to the Board, had they thought about it for a moment, that Brother Tasker's primary concern was not to convert the Church in the United States to his point of view, as one Board member charged. Rather, he was trying to save the "movement" in India from what was happening in America, due to the departure from many of the reformation principles which the Church of God had earlier espoused.

To be sure, he did reject what he saw as faulty biblical exegesis on the one hand and comeoutism–which he saw as sectarianism of the worst sort–on the other. These had no place in regions of the world where the great need was to cooperate, even pool resources to win "the heathen" to Christ. But the thing about hierarchical structuring of the movement and the accompanying loss of the freedom of the Spirit really got to him. That was bad enough. But to export it to the mission fields? That was nothing short of incredible. If the Anderson brethren wished to live with this utter anomaly, they should at least have the decency to keep it to themselves.

Which side, then, was wrong? Both were–but probably not in equal degree. In light of the growing strength and maturity of the Indian leadership of the movement in India (it seems from the beginning to have been that) and its own espoused "reformation principles," the Missionary Board must, I think, bear a major share of the blame. Yes, of course, this is all in retrospect. It's hindsight, something at which most of us are quite good—and I in particular.

This does not, however, exonerate the Board. But it does help us to get the record a bit straighter. They were faced with a difficult budget crisis and many local congregations were either doing or poised to do what they have done ever since when they have gotten out of sorts with "Anderson," that is, withhold funds. Under these circumstances, the Board had every reason to be sensitive concerning missionaries such as Brother Tasker, who were so far ahead of the rest of the Church. This may help explain why a few Missionary Board members who really did not want to voted for Brother Tasker's dismissal. The potential loss of income to the Board could have been devastating for the missionary cause.

All of those who supported Brother Tasker in what became the "Painful Separation" agree that things might have gone differently if he had taken a less vocal, less critical approach.[7] He was impatient, impetuous, and outspoken. Friends cautioned him, but he still sailed in with all flags flying and all guns blazing.

This was not just a question of differences of theological opinion to Brother Tasker, however—which he believed should never be allowed to "divide brethren," as he so eloquently argued in the "Withheld Letter" of 1923. Rather, he saw himself fighting a much larger battle, namely the right of the Indian Church to govern itself; and the freedom under the Spirit to inquire, argue, and differ in Christian love.

In the end, I think, everyone lost immeasurably. A.D. Khan, in a personal letter, concludes:

---

[7] A.D. Khan, for one, believed so. He says, "The thought occurs that death spared my father the anguish that the hapless incident would have occasioned, for his affection for the brethren in Anderson was sincere and his commitment to the faith of his choice deep. Possibly his nature, less abrupt than Tasker's would have exercised a moderating influence, who knows? My feeling is that unless the current trend of theological thinking in the Church in America eased up, it would not have been long before the parting of the ways came, involving regions not affected by G.P.T.'s departure" (personal letter, November 21, 1979). A.D. Khan confessed that in much of this—and particularly when it came to the theological questions in dispute in this case—he was no authority. His disclaimer is classic. "I am conscious of the limitations of my rather rambling reminiscing letter and its inadequacies. . . . I may even be guilty of pontifical pronouncements that are the special preserve of churchmen, on which laymen may poach only at their peril. If in these pages I have unwittingly been unduly critical of the Establishment in Anderson, I beg to be forgiven. This was not my intent."

I cannot but regard the move as unnecessary and unfortunate. I do not propose to present an apologia for Tasker's actions, but one should realize that his was an aggressive character, not inclined to take things lying down, and often intolerant of what he felt was wrong. With all his failings . . . his whole life was rooted in Christ and the propagation of the Christian faith. Obviously this was not deemed to be of much consequence in high places where the decisions were made. It was the age long conflict of authority and dissent. My view is . . . that greater restraint and imagination at this juncture would have given the course of events a happier turn. Granted that in a reformatory setting, confrontations of this kind may be expected and hard decisions have to be taken. Even so a verdict that forces a man of God out of the warmth of the community of saints must be deplored.

Perhaps "greater restraint and imagination" may have gone a long way to heal the breach. But, as I said in the beginning, I'm not at all convinced. Brother Tasker's friends may have been right. He was not just ahead of his times, but much too far ahead. So far, in fact, that the gap may have been virtually impossible to bridge at that point in our history. With the passing of time and the changing of the climate in the Church of God in America, he would be largely vindicated. But that was small comfort then.

As we will see, Brother Tasker was, even by the standards of his day, quite "orthodox" doctrinally—for the most part. But the points on which he differed with "the influential brethren" in Anderson were extremely critical in their minds. Eventually, the majority of the Church of God came to his views on those critical points, but in the teens and twenties of the 20th century, he was apparently, as I've said, too far ahead and too threatening to be tolerated.

## Chapter 4

## WHAT WERE HIS THEOLOGICAL VIEWS?

In the discussion prior to the passing of the Resolution which was intended to recall the Taskers from India, C.E. Brown asserted that he was convinced that Brother Tasker "does not believe the doctrines of this reformation." H.M. Riggle regally informed the Board that it took him "nine months to get rid of [Brother Tasker's teaching and its effects in Syria] and in fact some of the effects were never overcome. . . . Tasker's preaching in Syria was such that it took constant doctrinal preaching [on Riggle's part] to keep the church clean. . . . [Tasker's preaching] can bring people from heathenism. . . but only to a vague and hazy conception of Christianity generally" (Missionary Board Minutes, June 1924).

And finally, three other witnesses against Brother Tasker: J.W. Byers; F.G. Smith; and R.L. Berry. Brother Byers states that "Brother Tasker believes much as the Pentecostal movement and Christian Alliance people. He does not have a clear vision of the Church of God. It would be just as well to send a Christian Alliance missionary to India." According to F.G. Smith, "by leaving Tasker on the field, the Board is sanctioning liberalism . . . . we are in a measure taking the side of liberalism officially. . . . [His] attitude strikes at the operation of the Missionary Board in its efforts to teach and practice church government." And finally, Brother Berry: "If the Board had known [Tasker's] teachings on sanctification, they would not have sent him back to India."

Clearly, Brother Tasker was held both to be teaching *false* doctrine and failing to teach *true* doctrine, that is, the doctrine held by those in power in the Church of God—and with whom few dared to disagree publicly. But, unlike Brother Tasker, they kept their views to themselves and bided their time. Brother Tasker was thus seen by these most "influential brethren as a danger to "the movement" in India and in America, as well as in other countries. He had "departed from the faith." His views were dangerously heretical; he was an "apostate."

**Apostasy**

In an editorial in the *Gospel Trumpet* (January 22, 1925), entitled "Another Church Crisis at Hand," F.G. Smith likens Brother Tasker to: those in New Testament times who "departed from the faith or made superior claims;" to those involved in the "antisecond cleansing heresy;" and to those who became part of the fanatical and narrow Herald of Truth movement (under C.E. Orr). But "the true reformation" has always risen above these new movements aimed at bringing new truth to light in the church of God. Brother Smith laments:

> It is to be regretted that ministers sometimes permit themselves to become so blinded that in excessive zeal for their own conception of things they lose sight of some of the great underlying principles conditioning the special reformation work of God. Why should individuals so overrate themselves and their own importance as to imagine that if the work as a whole does not accept their interpretations and follow their leadership the cause must inevitably be lost?

**Out of Harmony**

Having established the "fact" that Brother Tasker was an apostate and was seeking to overthrow "God's great work of the final reformation of the church" which has been committed to the saints in the evening light, Brother Smith asserts: "Brother Tasker has long been entertaining doctrinal convictions out of harmony with what the reformation generally has been firmly convinced is the real teaching of the Word of God."

Brother Tasker is not a "narrow fanatic," he insists,

but just the opposite: an unbalanced and dangerous liberal, bent on diverting this reformation into some babylonish channel of his own making. He does not have the good of the movement at heart and the spirit that motivates him is some spirit other than the Spirit of God, who guides this great work of God. He claims to be the bearer of new light, but no new truth can emerge which is not in accordance with that which the movement has already received. He seeks, therefore, only to destroy that truth. Brother Smith continues:

> Under the guise of "liberty," "progress," and [now we have it] "local autonomy" some brethren who have been highly esteemed among us are now advocating principles quite at variance with those convictions which the great mass of our brethren believe they have received by the Spirit of God and which are vital to the welfare of this great work in which we are engaged. . . . We believe that this movement is a reformation of God, a movement divinely authorized and now being conducted by the Holy Spirit; hence we naturally inquire as to what spirit is getting hold of men who, while professing to believe this way, assume the attitude of opposers and faultfinders and apparently try with all their power to turn the work into other channels.

The *Gospel Trumpet* "Editorial" devotes considerable space also to a "Brother Fred Bruffet," who says that this movement, to be successful, must cooperate with other evangelical groups. "This can be done," he says, "in union evangelistic services, cooperative Sunday-school work, civic righteousness, and coordinated effort on the mission field." Further, we must "be willing to lose ourselves, our work, our all in a great and mighty move that will bring the whole church of God into cooperative unity." To which Brother Smith responds, "Shades of D.S. Warner!"

One might also respond—and, I think, semantically more correctly—"Shades of G. P. Tasker!" for Brother Tasker was saying almost the same thing in India, relating to the movement there. Small wonder the "influential brethren" were upset. But this was not the first time during their tenure that such "opposers" had arisen, nor would it by any means be the last.

While the editorial is concerned about "the many charges which Brother Tasker had launched against the Missionary Board" concerning "the manner of conducting our missionary work," its major concern seems to be to defend what are seen as cardinal and historic doctrines of "the movement." To challenge the Missionary Board on the question of its India policy is one thing; to challenge the *Gospel Trumpet* leadership on theological matters was, from their point of view, far more serious.

Besides, so they concluded, only because Brother Tasker was a theological "apostate" and "out of harmony" had he challenged the missions policies of the Board in the first place. Had he been doctrinally "straight" he would have accepted the Board's positions on most major issues without question. Doctrinal errors, in their view, led to all kinds of other errors. After all, the Holy Spirit could not fully lead anyone who rejected clear biblical truth.

Thus can Brother Smith assert that Brother Tasker was really questioning the Board on the issue of "church government" *as a doctrine*, not just as mission policy. If he were "in line" doctrinally with the movement and "in harmony" with the Board and the India Secretary of the Board, he would not be making a fuss about the policies now being pursued in the India mission. The very fact that he questioned Board policies was proof, so Brother Smith believed, that Brother Tasker was, at bottom, doctrinally "out of harmony" with those who were the divinely appointed "keepers of reformation truth."

We know that Brother Tasker's overriding concern—a concern that might well have reshaped his thinking on the question of church government—was the liberty and self-government of the movement in India under "the leadership of the Holy Spirit." He saw the liberty they had enjoyed from the beginning now being taken over by the Board and their agent in India, quite against the wishes of the Indian leaders themselves. Letters of protest were written by Brothers Khan and Nichols Roy, particularly, but to no avail. Brother Tasker "sided with [these] national leaders" against Brother Heinly and the Board–so the available correspondence reveals–further aggravating the situation.

But that was not likely what the "influential brethren" found so threatening and objectionable in Brother Tasker's sermons, writings, and private conversations and which eventually–and inevitably, in my view–led to his dismissal (for which the euphemism "recall" was used) from missionary service under the Missionary Board. Just exactly what was he saying that created so much fuss among the "brethren" and at least some congregations in the United States? To that question we now turn.

### Basic Theological Views

Generally, Brother Tasker held to the evangelical doctrine of his day, as did the Church of God generally. Like the Church of God as a whole, he accepted classical (Calvinist) Protestant doctrines such as the Lordship of Christ, the authority and finality of Scripture, justification by grace through faith, the necessity of repentance and the new birth, the power of the Holy Spirit in the life of the believer, the necessity of preaching the gospel to all nations, the second coming of Christ, and the resurrection and final judgment.

He also accepted the specific views of the Church of God on the Kingdom of God as a present spiritual reality, rather than a future, millennial kingdom, the church as the redeemed and wholly-sanctified people of God, the freedom and sovereignty of the Spirit in the governance of the church, the evils of sectarianism and division, and the ultimate sinfulness of ecclesiastical structure–particularly hierarchical structure–in the life of the church. He preached, taught, and wrote these views with great enthusiasm, skill, and conviction–and continued to do so until the end of his life.

What, then, was the problem? What doctrines of "this reformation" did he not accept? Essentially, only one: the doctrine of the church of God reformation movement as God's restoration of the true church, heavenly Zion, under the inspiration and guidance of the Holy Spirit, according to the Scriptures. Into this great and holy church, that is, the church of God, God was gathering his true children, bringing them home from sect Babylon. All who refused to attend this great wedding feast and to honor the Bride of the Lamb were lost and condemned forever.

In other words, you had to accept this truth, repent, come out of Babylon (all forms of Christianity except "this reformation movement"), and submit yourself entirely to the spiritual authority of those whom God has chosen and gifted to be in charge of you. This was the only way you could be saved and thus inherit eternal life.[2] "This movement," F.G. Smith confidently asserted, is "divinely authorized and conducted by the Holy Spirit." To say the same of any other group is heresy–and Brother Tasker was certainly saying you could be saved in one or another of the so-called sects of Babylon, remain in that "sect," and still be saved.

To be sure, he did not accept the view of the "influential brethren" gathered around Brother Smith on the question of sanctification–and very probably a number of other things. He considered many of their views on a variety of theological and biblical subjects to be narrow, rigid, and uninformed, or the product of poor reasoning or exegesis.

Under other circumstances, the question of sanctification might have created considerably more furor than it appears from the record to have done. It surely did on other occasions with a number of others. However, in this case, the "influential brethren" seem to have had more

---

[2] This may appear, at first glance, as something of an overstatement. I think, however, that it can be argued inferentially on the basis of many statements in early *Gospel Trumpet* articles, letters, and testimonies that those who heard this "complete gospel" and did not respond by "coming out" were "lost and Hellbound." Later, it occurred to some of the Evening Light Saints (H.M Riggle for example) that an exception needed to be made to cover those who would never have the opportunity to hear this "great truth." Brother Tasker often insisted that people could be saved without ever having heard of the Church of God (Anderson, Indiana). To assert that seems to me to suggest that one is seeking to contradict a "real" view, not a "fictitious" one. One does not battle a doctrine that no one proclaims.

important issues on the table.

Brother Berry was sure that if Brother Tasker's views on the subject had been known to the Board in 1921, they surely would not have sent him back to India. I question that the Board did not know. Neither Brother Khan nor Brother Nichols Roy accepted the Anderson view of sanctification and, if it was known that Brother Tasker "sided with" the Indian leaders, the Board would have known from that alone.

I suspect that the doctrine of sanctification weighed more heavily in Brother Berry's view than it did in anyone else's—except, perhaps, Brother Riggle's. It is not highly likely, even at that point in our history, that it would have moved the Board to dismiss Brother Tasker from missionary service, even though they would have tried—unsuccessfully, I'm sure—to convince him otherwise.

But to reject the Church's view of itself as the sole result of God's final restoration of the pure Gospel was apostasy from the faith. It was the most dangerous of liberalisms. It struck at the very foundation of the great Truth God had given to this movement. To strike at this was to strike at the ecclesial authority of those who were the chief guardians and heralds of this Truth. If that authority could not be upheld, "this movement" would crumble to dust.

On March 5, 1923, J.W. Phelps, Secretary Treasurer of the Missionary Board wrote to Brother Tasker summing it all up in these words:

> . . . the gist of all the charges is that your sermons, your missionary lectures, your private conversations, and your general attitude toward the church have in them so much unbalanced liberalism that they widen out the boundaries of this reformation until, to use the words of Brother Smith, "like a river in the desert without banks it spreads until it loses itself in the sand where it evaporates, and nothing is left but the barren desert of denominationalism."

## The Church of God

What, in Brother Tasker's view, was this entity called "the church of God?" Was it co-extensive and co-terminus with the "reformation movement" having its general offices in Anderson, Indiana, and publishing the *Gospel Trumpet*? No, said he, that is the Church of God (capital C), not the church of God (lower case c) spoken of in the New Testament. To assume that these are one and the same thing is not only mistaken, but dangerously and grievously mistaken. Its end result could only be sectarianism as narrow as any sectarianism in existence.

### Another Denomination?

Brother Tasker was convinced that this was, in fact, what had happened to the Church of God. What may have begun as a movement, he believed, had become another denomination, with much of the structure and "machinery" of any denomination. (And high on the list was missionary boards that made rules and regulations for national churches and field secretaries who imperialistically enforced them.) Ecclesiasticism had taken over as surely as it had in any of the groups the Church of God referred to as "sect Babylon." Thus, insisting that they were "the church of God" spoken of in the New Testament was totally unacceptable to him.

"Any student of the Bible," he asserted, "ought to know that neither in truth nor in Scripture is 'church of God' a denominational designation at all. It is not a name any more than the word 'family' is. . . . It is a phrase designating *status*, the status of all Christians, that they who once were merely God's *creatures* are now his chosen ones, his *ekklesia*, or *church*" (*An Appeal to the Free and Autonomous Churches of Christ in the Fellowship of the Evening Light*, 1924, p.9, hereinafter referred to as *An Appeal*).

These "chosen ones," he believed, were to be found in all denominations of the Christian faith, not just in the Church of God (Anderson, Indiana). Yes, he said, we are part of that church of God spoken of in Scripture, but only a very small part. The great bulk of it is to be found beyond our boundaries.

No, said Brother Phelps in the exchange of correspondence, "The heart of the whole matter is that this organization of which we are a part is the church of God" (*An Appeal*, p.11). Brother Tasker could not accept this. He replied, the Church of God is "a *very small part* of the real church of God. I certainly don't want to be guilty of trying to put GOD'S reformation into any such box as that" (*An Appeal*, p. 24).

So, after all, he did believe in God's reformation, that God was at work completing the mighty work he had begun centuries before. Brother Tasker says as much in a lengthy doctrinal statement to the Missionary Board—in italics yet.

> . . . *God's reform is a movement of the Spirit of God in this one body which is destined to bring its present earthly members into right and intelligent relationship to one another in Christ, so that the Church's spiritual and fundamental unity may have its proper outward expression everywhere throughout the world and that her great evangelistic mission in the earth may be furthered* . . . (*An Appeal*, p. 24).

Here Brother Tasker is not referring to the Church of God (Anderson, Indiana), that is "Church" as opposed to "church," in spite of his capitalization of church (whether his mistake or his printer's, I am not prepared to say). This understanding, he believed, summarized both Brother Warner's original position—before he began to be enamored with what he saw as biblical "prophecy"—and what should be the position of the Church which sprang from him.

But, so he goes on to say, when we turned to this "geographical comeoutism," in effect, we betrayed God's reformation. "Yes," he hastens to say, "we have been sincere, for the real heart of the work is sound. But being conscientious and sincere has not made us right in transgressing a fundamental law of the kingdom of heaven" (*An*

*Appeal, p. 28).* God's *true* reformation brings born-again Christians *together,* not necessarily *out.*

Clearly, Brother Tasker did not agree at all with the direction "the movement" was being taken by the "influential brethren" in Anderson. You believe, he said to the Board, that *"we* are 'nucleus,' 'vanguard,' 'refuge,' 'rendevous,' 'center,' and so forth . . . ." He concludes:

Our Lord's whole attitude and teachings were all calculated to destroy any such notion of rank and preference or precedence among Christians. For him to say that his followers are "the light of the world" and for John to declare that "we (Christians) are of God and the whole world lies in the evil one," are very different things from saying to *some* Christians that they are the light in contradistinction to *other* Christians–the center and rendevous for all other believers to gather to (*An Appeal,* p. 25).

The claim that "we" are the church of God, heavenly Jerusalem, Zion on earth, is a blind and narrow conceit that has turned truly spiritual people away from us. It is "an offence to thousands of genuine Christian people and is the chief cause of our not being many times more numerous than we are today." Here Brother Tasker's directness, even bluntness, shows through. But Brother Phelps had asked for an open and frank statement, hadn't he? I can imagine that the following words caused no little agitation and headshaking among the Board members:

I may perhaps be the practical center of a gathering of God, but as soon as I become self-conscious of it, *so that I have to rise up and defend the idea that I am,* it is a dead sure sign that I have ceased to be if I ever was. My very attitude, which is only the fruit of an idea, utterly disqualifies me for such a position in the minds of spiritual people, and I will soon be left alone to my claims. When any man (or any movement) really gets to believing that the only seat for him (or it) is the front seat, the time of the rejection of that man (or movement) is at hand. Self-importance and spiritual pride are the prelude of sure rejection. God will have none of that in His Kingdom (*An Appeal,* pp. 25-26, author's italics).

Brother Tasker certainly did not reject the name, "Church of God," or the fellowship that so designated itself. To the end of his days, he considered himself to be part of this fellowship. In effect, however, he was eventually cut off from the Church of God in India, but in retirement in Canada he associated with a Church of God congregation and preached in others. But, true to his theological convictions and the habit of many years, he refused to confine himself to those associations.

However, the Church of God certainly had its place in the kingdom of God, he believed. But it should never think that place is pre-eminent, "in the front seat," as he puts it. Preeminence of place is reserved for Christ alone, not for any segment of his followers. The notion that we are "heavenly Jerusalem" or earthly "Zion" and that all the world must come to us is a vain conceit. True seekers may come to Christ and attain his fullness without ever knowing of the group calling themselves "Church of God." Nor would their personal allegiance to Christ necessarily be strengthened or their spirituality deepened by becoming a part of the Church of God (Anderson, Indiana). (Where this would be the case, Brother Tasker was quite in favor of such people coming to the Church of God—or to any other Church where the Gospel of Christ was faithfully proclaimed and lived out.)

This self-conscious assertion of preeminence agitated him deeply. The constant emphasis upon ourselves, our self-consciousness, as he expressed it in one of his marginal notes, was an offense to the Lordship of Christ and the kingdom of God. He wanted none of it. (This reminds me of a comment made some years ago by an older friend following our then-called "International Convention of the Church of God: "For the first time in my memory, more was said in this campmeeting about Christ than about the Church of God." Brother Tasker would have been in wholehearted approval of that!)

But Brother Tasker wasn't finished yet with his "front seat" metaphor. He goes on to spin it out even further:

And why, I might add, has there always been such an ado on our part, from the days of poor G.P. Keeling until now, to preserve this front seat for ourselves? Is the first place so much the only place for us in the onward march of the kingdom of God that we cannot preserve our identity unless we sit in it? Hear then the word of the Lord: "The first shall be last and the last first" (p. 29).

## Calling People to Christ

This forthright statement of convictions was certainly not designed to smooth ruffled feathers in high places, but it seems, at this point, that Brother Tasker was no longer concerned about that. If we are what we claim to be, he contends, then we will never ask how anyone stands in relation to this "movement," but how he stands in relation to Christ. We are to call people to Christ, not to "this movement." If they come freely to us and wish to join us, that is different than our dogmatic insistence that they must come to us if they are to escape "the mark of the Beast" and burning in Hell–one of the inferences Brother Tasker drew from F.G. Smith's book, *Revelation Explained*—with which he most emphatically disagreed.

Paul's great ambition, he continues, was to form Christ in believers and present them as a pure bride to Christ." If we talked as much about Christ as he did," he contends, "not as a doctrine but just because we were full of Christ, as he was, don't you think people might find it easier to believe we are His bride?" A bride, he says, is "never the center of things." Rather, it is the Bridegroom.

He adds, "Brother Warner, I think, caught that vision. They say he was full of Christ. I could also think so from many of his hymns. They breathe Christ-consciousness. And his preaching against sectarianism and deadness and man-rule he found in the Church of his time and place was needed, and the need is not past by any means" (*An Appeal,* p. 27).

In other words, those who are truly a part of the great church of God are deeply Christ-conscious. That church, as his bride, is centered on him. It thinks not of itself and its exalted position, but of the Lord alone. It witnesses to him; it calls others to him, not to itself. That the Church of God speaks so much of itself, its doctrines, its experiences, and insists that it, and it among all others, knows the mind of God, that it exclusively is the ark of salvation, is sure evidence that it does not know its place in the Kingdom of God. One concluding quotation:

> We may know for an absolute certainty what the Holy Ghost is gathering to in GOD'S last reformation, by what He gathered to in the first one, and by what he will gather to at the end of time. "Our gathering together is unto HIM" (2 Thess. 2:1), not to doctrines and experiences, or works of grace, or even to "the one church," however true and necessary those conceptions may be *in their right place*, as living, glorious, compelling, conquering Personality. Blessed be His adorable Name forever and ever (p. 26)!

## Coming Out of Babylon and Sectism

Given Brother Tasker's view of the church of God, in contrast to the view of the "influential brethren" in Anderson who were seeking to get him "into line," it then follows that he would reject their "comeoutism." The absolute necessity of "coming out of Babylon," they claimed, was the view of "the vast majority" of the "movement"–represented, of course, by the several "influential brethren"—and undoubtedly even an influential sister or two.[3] (However, E.A. Reardon, for one, did not

---

[3] Whether "the vast majority" of the Church of God in every geographical region actually held this view even in the mid-1920s is debatable. Nonetheless, given the eclipse that was to happen to the come-out doctrine in the next decade or two, it seems to me reasonable to believe that many questions and reservations existed long before 1924.

accept this view. He was quite sure that at "the grassroots" many were much more inclusive than this—or so he suggests in A Message to Young Ministers.)

D.S. Warner was, so Brother Tasker believed, doubtless right in "coming out" of his sectarian association (actually, I think, he was thrown out), but that doesn't mean he was right in everything he did and said. When he began to interpret prophecy in terms of "geographical comeoutism," the change in his attitude and spirit was remarkable—or so Brother Tasker concluded from reading Warner's "biography" (that is, Birth of a Reformation, A.L. Byers, 1921).

The great focus of Brother Warner's ministry from that point on was calling people out of sect Babylon—a practice that seems to have deeply alienated his second wife, Sarah Keller Warner, who subsequently took a very strong stand against his "sectarian" teaching. Much to the dismay—and, perhaps, embarrassment—of those in "the movement," she published her views in April, 1884 in The Christian Harvester, a holiness journal of that period, for the whole Holiness Movement to read. (To which Brother Warner responded indignantly in the Gospel Trumpet, denouncing, even demonizing, her in two lengthy articles.) Brother Tasker asks,

> But is there no truth to what his poor dear wife wrote . . . . "It (this effort to unite God's people by calling them out of the churches) simply cuts off a few members by themselves, who get an idea that none are clearly sanctified unless they see as 'we' do; and, then, they have a harsh grating that is the very opposite of love. I have found that the predominant spirit of the comeout movement is the same self-righteous, pharisaical spirit that Christ rebuked when he was here on earth." So she spoke. Some truth in it, I think (An Appeal, pp 32).

## Sectarianism

What resulted, in Brother Tasker's view, was a sect more sectarian than the various "sects" out of which its members came. This is a statement I recall hearing him make on numerous occasions. In *An Appeal*, he declares quite emphatically that he is against sectarianism in any form. It is, he says, "Christ-obscuring, ignoble, and sinful." But what has resulted from the comeoutism of Brother Warner and his associates–and those who have followed in their train–is an attitude and spirit that can only be called sectarian. In fact, he exclaims, "I tell you only the sober truth when I say that the people of the most sectarian mind and attitude that I have ever met in all my life have been just those people who have most fully imbibed our doctrine and spirit of geographical comeoutism" (*An Appeal*, p. 31).

He believed, with deep and passionate conviction, that true spiritual Christians were to be found in all denominations–even if not in great numbers in some cases at least. It was often good for them to remain right where they were, he said, as salt and leaven, witnessing to the fullness of Christ in their lives. The effects on less-enlightened Christians could be great indeed.

Brother Tasker was aware, of course, that they could not always do so. Brother Warner, after all, had not been able to, since he had, in effect, been "defrocked" by the Churches of God (Winebrennarian) for his strong holiness views and his practice of freedom in the Spirit, which had led him to establish an unauthorized congregation. Nor had the Methodists, in the end, been able to remain within the Anglican Church. Brother Tasker's words again:

> *I believe in the ultimate necessity of coming out of all associations formally organized by vote or informally organized by sentiment, where the word of God is not honored, where his gospel is not preached and obeyed, and where his Spirit is quenched in believers* (*An Appeal*, p. 31).

. . . . . . . . . . . . . . . . . . . . . . . . . . . . . . . . . . . . . . . . .

Positive preaching of the kind that will ENTHRONE CHRIST and draw men into the realization of his abiding life and activity within them, is simply bound of itself to produce a true Christian Church and all the "coming out" that may be necessary. It was not the preaching of "separation" that made the saints one on Pentecost and after, but the getting them filled with the Holy Ghost (*An Appeal*, p. 35*).*

In F.G. Smith's book, *The Last Reformation*, Brother Tasker found a statement which, he said, "ought to have been put in capital letters." It is this: "The fundamental error underlying all other errors on this subject (that of Church organization and government) was the idea of *an absent Christ.*"

To this, he responds: "If we are ever to get at the root of the errors and cure the evil of the thing for the people of God still involved in hurtful ecclesiasticisms, must we not work to awaken within their hearts and minds the sense of *a present Christ?*" Calling them out of existing systems is "of little use" unless we first call them to the fullness of Christ. In order to do this, we must, he insists, "go where they are and mix with them" (for which he was, apparently, being quite severely criticized).

Simply to call people to separate themselves from the denomination where they are without first making the fullness of Christ known to them was unbiblical in his view. Neither Jesus nor his apostles deliberately separated themselves from the Jewish people. Eventually separation came, but not until the new wine had burst the old wine skins. Calling people out, Brother Tasker contended, "without first bringing them the sense of *this present Christ*, simply makes more sectarianism. The *label* only is different" (*An Appeal*, p. 34).

It seems to me Brother Tasker was really insisting that the true church of God was precisely a movement *within* Christendom whose primary objective was not to "come out," but to make Christ present in the Churches. If all who were experiencing the fullness of Christ "came out," then no one would be left to witness to that fullness *from within.* And, given the denominational barriers of the day in the Christian world, outside voices would go largely unheeded. All comeoutism really does, then, is create an isolated community of comeouters who can no longer effectively witness within the groups out of which they came.

While, to Brother Tasker, this logic seemed inescapable, it had apparently escaped his interlocutors.

Thus Church of God and church of God were two different
entities—even thought he believed that the Church of God
(Anderson) was, in the main, part of that true biblical
church of God. But it was held in the powerful grip of a
sectarian spirit—among its leaders, at least. Repentance
of and cleansing from this sectarianism was certainly
necessary if it were to become even more a part of God's
great church.

Brother Tasker was especially convinced that this
sectarian approach to missionary work in India was wrong.
It is here that he could wax prophetically eloquent—as the
following statement illustrates:

> New missionaries come from you determined that
> *they* are not going to "build up sectism," but they
> have to be mighty careful or they will introduce
> really *more* sectarianism into the minds of their
> charges than there is in any part of the Christian
> body here. The *name* "Church of God" does not
> sanctify the spirit of separation and alienation. The
> question which intelligent, *thoughtful* Indian
> Christians ask at once is, "Why, are we not church
> of God? Into what then did we come, into what
> were we inducted when we became Christians,
> when we came to Christ and were baptized?" Such
> men will never come to US as nucleus, or refuge,
> or rendevous. Never. What is an individual (and
> usually a disgruntled individual), here and there, to
> the whole body of the Indian Christian Church (*An
> Appeal*, p. 36)?

Make no mistake about it, Brother Tasker passionately
disliked sectarianism, no matter where it might be found,
whether in "sect Babylon" or among those who claimed to
have "come out" of all such associations. He often
preached vigorously against the notion that one must
belong to this or that group to be "saved." What saved one
was being "in Christ" and certainly no Christian group held
a monopoly on that. Salvation, so Brother Tasker believed,
was by the grace of God through faith in Christ, not by
belonging to this or that Church. Wherever faith in Christ

was to be found, there was salvation.

But his ire could really rise to remarkable heights when confronting sectarianism among the people he had chosen as his own. "Think of it!," he writes to the Missionary Board. "What is possessing you? Did you not read your Secretary's letter? 'This movement (meaning ourselves), the heavenly Jerusalem of Scripture.' *At this rate, if you really mean what you are saying, you will soon be out-Roming Rome itself*" (*An Appeal,* p. 37, italics mine).

In an earlier letter, the "Secretary," Brother Phelps, had, perhaps unwisely, attempted to persuade Brother Tasker by prooftexting from scripture that the "come out" doctrine was necessary and reasonable. He had, apparently, not learned that when fighting a dangerous foe you do not choose his favorite field of battle or take up the weapons with which he is most highly skilled. The "proof text" was, of course, 2 Corinthians 6:14, 17: "Be ye not unequally yoked together with unbelievers." And, "Come ye out from among them and be ye separate."

In his reply, Brother Tasker remarks quite forthrightly: "A man who has worked any length of time among the heathen, for example . . . would never be guilty of applying [this text] to PROFESSING CHRISTIANS!. . . . They are NOT unbelievers in the Scripture sense of the word at all." The related verse, verse 17 of the same text, should not be applied to Christian believers either. "It is Christ and Belial, the temple of God and idols, a believer and an unbeliever, that are the antithesis here, not professing Christians of differing degrees of spiritual enlightenment" (*An Appeal,* p. 17). End of the lesson in basic biblical exegesis!

### *Inter-denominationalism*

One of Brother Tasker's major sins, in the view of the Anderson "brethren," was his refusal to preach to those of "sect Babylon," whether in India or North America, that to receive the fullness of Christ they must "come out" of all sectarian associations and into the fellowship of the "church of God." To fail to preach this was to fail to preach "the Gospel" in its revealed fullness. Brother Phelps, writing on behalf of the Missionary Board, informs Brother Tasker of some of the charges against him:

> . . . others report that there is not in your messages enough of the vital saving power of the old-time gospel; others are to the effect that in your talks there is not enough differentiation between the Church of God and denominations. . . . Then there are some reports from points in missionary countries that the message is too vague and lacks that vital, dynamic, life-giving force of the real gospel (*An Appeal,* p. 5).

Brother Tasker's reply, I think, indicates the extent of the distance between his thinking and that of the Missionary Board. Reports such as these, he wrote to Brother Phelps, are "too trifling and absurd for the notice of sensible people." He preached Christ "and him crucified." That is the "old-time gospel." That is the "real gospel." It is that gospel and only that gospel that is the "vital, dynamic, life-giving force" needed in India or anywhere else. "Threshing Babylon" and "rescuing" a few "kernels" here and there has little to do with the gospel of Christ as recorded in Scripture. It may, in fact, be a perversion of it.

The refusal to preach "comeoutism," however, was compounded by the fact that Brother Tasker was actually cooperating with "sect Babylon," preaching and teaching in their churches, joining with them in cooperative evangelistic efforts, and benefiting them in other ways—none of which really benefited the Church of God. Doubtless he is able to persuade some to "come out of heathenism," someone said, but most of these are lost to the Church of God anyway, so he is really of no value to us as a missionary.

Brother Tasker's student work in Calcutta was just such a venture. It was not building up the Church of God and was of little importance, certainly not worthy of the support of the Missionary Board—so another member calmly announced. We had better dismiss him, so our money can be put to use building up "this movement."

But of even greater concern to some of the Board

members was Brother Tasker's involvement in "inter-denominational" evangelistic and humanitarian efforts. It is these interdenominational efforts, F.G. Smith wrote, that are the ultimate expression of "liberalism"–a term, which it seems, he was attempting to elevate into a major "red flag" label. In an editorial (*Gospel Trumpet*, May 15, 1924) he says:

Today since it is becoming rather popular for religious leaders to decry the divisions of Christendom, a host of pseudo-reformers are to be found who talk and preach against sectarian divisions but who have never made the journey to Zion themselves nor learned the first principles of *concord, unity, submission*, and persevering effort required to restore Zion. Interdenominational effort is their only remedy for sectarianism. They pretend to be out of Babylon, but as a matter of fact their success depends almost entirely upon their ability to get Babylonians to work together, while temporarily ignoring their differences. To those of us who have long ago become established in Zion and have discerned the true work of God in the *substantial upbuilding* of his kingdom on real New Testament lines, all such union efforts, which leave the converts to drift directly into the sects, are nothing but unworthy Babylon compromises, and we can never have fellowship with such schemes (italics mine).

Brother Tasker sputtered in indignation at what he saw as "spiritual pride and arrogance." It was, so he believed, precisely what sanctification was supposed to eliminate from the heart and mind of the true believer. At this point, I doubt, however, that the editorial was intended to sound quite as prideful and arrogant as it seems to. But the language is incautious and certainly could be read that way. (A certain pride and arrogance, I think, naturally adheres to the conviction that we are the chosen ones, we are right, we are the mediators of God's final truth to the world—no matter how deeply we feel that we are only being properly grateful and humble.)

Brother Smith was not yet finished, however. "It means something to be out of Babylon. The saint who has been in that contaminated atmosphere needs not only to see the evils of the system and come out, but he needs, so to speak, to be washed, and scrubbed and fumigated–until all the defilement and the very scent of Babylon have been swept away by the Spirit of the living God."

To Brother Smith, the principle was very simple: "If Babylon is wrong . . . then interdenominationalism is no better." In fact, he said, "sects thrive on interdenominational efforts." Of course, the sects have in them some "honest souls," who have responded to "the degree of light God has given them." But the work of the Holy Spirit, "known to us for years," is to bring them out of Babylon into the one true body of Christ, "and there governs them peaceably according to the principles of the divine theocracy."

He asserts, even more emphatically, that anyone [and probably especially Brother Tasker and those who agreed with him] whose work is "interlocked" with the "sect system" has one foot "in Babylon." If that is the case, then "we know full well that [he] *does not have the other foot in Zion.* THE TWO PLACES ARE TOO FAR APART TO PERMIT OF SUCH A RELATION." Those who attempt it, get "lost in the fog." They have drunk the wine of Babylon and have lost their vision of "the precious unity of saints being effected through the clear teaching of this reformation." Those who do not "stand on the heights of Zion and proclaim the message of God, '*Come out* of her, my people,'" but seek to work interdenominationally, "carry so much of the scent of Babylon that it is becoming a stench in the nostrils of many good, righteous saints of God who have been keeping clear themselves."

Now, I can certainly understand Brother Tasker reacting very strongly in the first place to such a "sectarian" statement as this. It made neither biblical nor practical sense to him. In missions, to preach comeoutism could only work great mischief for all concerned. He insisted that Christians in India were such a tiny minority in such a great sea of "heathenism" that they could not afford to exclude and alienate one another. To do so was both to contradict the gospel of Christ and to remain small, insignificant, and powerless in the face of such crying spiritual need. Working cooperatively made good sense. From the beginning, the "true fathers" of the Church of God in India had so worked with other churches and mission groups, as had Brother Tasker himself. It was the only course at that time that made scriptural or practical sense to them. Geographical comeoutism made no biblical or theological sense anywhere, at the best of times, but in "heathen lands" it was incredibly bad mission strategy.

The Missionary Board's India Secretary faithfully sought to put the lid on all such cooperative practice with other mission groups–at least until he himself became an evangelistic missionary in what is now Bangladesh. This led to instant friction between him and Brother Tasker. It was bad enough to demand that he get the Secretary's approval before accepting any speaking engagements, but to demand the same of the Indian leaders was the last straw. This was galling indeed!

Apparently, Brother Heinly took his "commission" very seriously–at least in the beginning. But such practices led to Brother Khan's death (in Brother Tasker's view—whether or not that view could be substantiated medically), the removal of the Taskers as missionaries of the Church of God, the resignation of others of the mission staff, and the eventual disaffection of Brother Nichols Roy and the churches he had established. As Lester Crose said, the results were disastrous for everyone involved: the Indian church; the India mission; and the Missionary Board.

## Conclusion

Brother Tasker's strong view of the New Testament church of God as consisting of all those whom God had called out of the world and into Christ made it impossible for him to accept any view of the church such as that which he thought was being insisted upon by Brother Smith and other "influential brethren." The very notion that any exclusive body of people who thought of themselves as God's Holy Remnant, the true saints of God, Zion, the heavenly Jerusalem, and the called out people of the evening light, alone constituted that church was, in his words, "utter nonsense."

In the first place, it was an unbiblical notion based on "obscure texts" isolated from their contexts. The general force of scripture "properly interpreted" [a statement with which I have great difficulty–after all, who is to say what's "proper?"] makes such a view untenable. Much of Brother Smith's view was expressed in *Revelation Explained,* (written 1906, published 1908) about which Brother Tasker wrote to Brother Smith at length in 1921, questioning his methods of interpreting apocalyptic literature, especially interpreting it as "prophecy." One simply could not, Brother Tasker insisted, build such a great theological edifice on a book so notoriously difficult to interpret, not when the interpretation contradicted the plain sense of the New Testament in general.

It is not clear what occasioned the letter. (A letter, by the way, which would not have further endeared Brother Tasker to Brother Smith!) But, whatever the occasion, Brother Smith apparently had no wish to debate what he considered "revealed" truth. What had come from God was beyond dispute.

Brother Tasker's deep conviction was that the church of God was a "state," a spiritual reality, a "family" of true (born-again) believers, gathered unto Christ and learning how to be wholly submitted to him, and governed by the Holy Spirit. The believers were scattered throughout the various groups and denominations–including the Church of God. They were one in Christ, one in faith, one in mission. Since this was the case, recognizing them wherever they were found, working unitedly with them in preaching Christ was the proper Christian thing to do.

Besides, he believed, unity could never be realized through uniformity of belief and practice imposed by some "ecclesiastical authority" purporting to be the direct channel of "divine theocracy." (Thus Brother Tasker's comment that the Anderson brethren were in danger of "out-Roming Rome itself.") It was only natural that from country to country beliefs and practices would differ somewhat anyway. Unity, then, could only be a *spiritual* unity in Christ. To attempt to force Indians to think and act as Americans was a violation of true oneness.

It was best in the case of India, therefore, to let the particular "genius" of Indian Christians show through by allowing them to do what they had been doing from the beginning, govern themselves, rather than insisting that they must march to the beat of an American drum. The Missionary Board's position was quite different, however. Without an American drum, only chaos and confusion could result. "Even under the most favorable circumstances," Brother Phelps wrote, "the Indian mind, brilliant, analytical, theoretical, impractical, is sadly in need of the strong, positive, aggressive, emphatic, decisive thought of the West" (*An Appeal,* p. 11).

Brother Tasker could not, would not, accept such views. They made no sense to him biblically–his first and most important filter–and even less sense in terms of mission policy and missionary practice. Here we have the proverbial irresistible force meeting the immovable object– from which the only result can be immeasurable friction. The end of it all could not be long in coming–unless, of course, someone gave in. At this point, at least, it appears that no one did.

## Chapter 5

## WHERE DID IT ALL END?

It appears from our story thus far, I think, that Brother Tasker and the "influential brethren" of the Missionary Board and the Gospel Trumpet Company may simply have been too far apart to continue working together. It was, for the Board, a question of control: who controlled the Church in India; who controlled the work of Church of God missionaries in India; and, it seems, who controlled what they preached.

Both Brother Tasker and the Indian leaders, who had begun the work in India independently of the Church in America, were convinced that the Indian Church and the Church in America should work together in "fraternal" relationship. The "influential brethren" in Anderson would have none of it–particularly since the Indian leaders were not sounding forth the clarion call to complete separation from all Babylonish sects, but were, in fact, cooperating with them on many fronts.

Brother Tasker also felt strongly that Church of God missionaries should continue to work in collegial relationship with the Board, under the leadership of the Holy Spirit, as they had done from the beginning. The "influential brethren" would have none of that either. It was not that he did not believe in accountability, but believed it must be mutual.

What the "influential brethren" had in mind was a structure that was both hierarchical and paternalistic. That was not, however, what they thought they were thinking. After all, they didn't believe in organization. Only a sect committed that disgusting sin. They believed they were simply organizing the *work* of the "movement" to achieve greater accountability and to assure that Brother Tasker and the Indian leaders "got in line" and stayed there.

But Brother Tasker and the Indian leaders saw this as "ecclesiasticism" and fought against it. It was a denial of the reformation principles on which the Indian work was built. Further proof of this ecclesiasticism was the establishment of Boards and the attempts to centralize the work of the Church around the world in Anderson, Indiana. This was clearly, in their view, "man rule."

They saw the imposition of a Field Secretary on the Church in India as even more alarming evidence of this "man rule." One of the Field Secretary's primary assignments, in Brother Tasker's words, was to get the field workers so busy doing "proper Church of God things" that they wouldn't have time for involvement with Babylon. Particularly was he to "harness up" Brother Khan for the Church of God and so prevent him from accepting "invitations to go other places." The Field Secretary "strained every muscle of his ingenious organizing brain" to assure that this happened. Brother Tasker's writes:

> I sympathized with Brother Heinly's difficulty, but I did not share his viewpoint and opinion in this matter. They certainly were not charismatic. It is true that Brother Khan's gifts had but small scope amongst us here. We had not the field for him, but GOD had, and we had the honor (and the expense) of having the man. As Dr. Howells, the Principal of Serampore College . . . said to me the day of the funeral, "Why, *that* man belonged to the whole church." He did, though he happened to be entrusted to our care (*An Appeal*, p. 38).

What agitated Brother Tasker particularly in all of this was that "we talked charismatic government at home but on the field . . . we acted man-rule."

And so the die was cast. Each side in the debate appears to have made its decision and seemed not to be willing to compromise, for the sake of "conscience." More letters and more thrusts and counter-thrusts simply hardened their resolve. They were, so it seemed, at an impasse, so the Missionary Board settled the question by using their financial power. The Taskers were "recalled" and their support terminated after six months.

## The Independent Years

In the June, 1924 Annual Meeting of the Missionary Board, two or three members voiced the opinion that if "recalled," the Taskers would refuse to leave India and would find some other way of supporting themselves. They were right. Brother Tasker later wrote: "We certainly feel no call from the Lord to forsake the work He has given us to do here and go home . . . in the middle of our term, which was begun with the Board's approval and with them fully cognizant of our present views" (*An Appeal*, p. 2).

E. E. Byrum was convinced that whether or not Brother Tasker was recalled, he would remain in India and go ahead with his work. If not recalled, he would continue to "spread his poison" in the name of the Board. If recalled, he would stay in India and work "under the auspices of some other missionary society."

The Taskers did stay in Calcutta and continued in the same kind of evangelistic and teaching work they had been doing under the Board. But they did not work "under the auspices" of any other society. They decided, instead, to work independently of any board or society, simply trusting God to supply their needs from other sources. This was a bold move, but probably consistent with Brother Tasker's general theological convictions. He would, from that point on, be supported by "the church of God."

Much later, he wrote of this decision, describing it as one that brought a great sense of happiness and freedom. Or, in his words, "an almost overwhelming realization of the joy and presence of the Lord, when one day he and. . . Minnie solemnly covenanted before God to put Him and His leadership before the approval and wishes of men" (Thaddeus Neff, *Our Missionaries*, p. 30).

They could not, of course, continue to work with the Church of God, as they had been doing, but it is not likely that they broke off all contact. Indian leaders in eastern India were his trusted friends, but if they had continued to call upon him for help and counsel, the support they received from the Board would have been threatened.

Brother Heinly would have had to see to that. Besides, Brother Tasker would not have wanted to put his dear brothers in that kind of situation. His only alternative was to "stay in Calcutta"–but welcome them warmly when they came calling at his door. Brother and Sister Nichols Roy were, however, quite a different case. Subsequently, they also followed Brother Tasker's lead and broke off their relationship with the Missionary Board, declaring themselves free from this new sectism and the bonds of its financial support. They were no longer concerned, to paraphrase Brother Tasker, about who had "the key to the money chest." Their relationship with him continued much as it had before.

### An Appeal

But, as A.D. Khan said, Brother Tasker was not one to take what he believed to be wrong lying down. He believed he had friends and supporters in the United States who would support him and his wife if they knew what was really going on and why they were being dismissed. It seems that Fred Bruffett, who shared the limelight with Brother Tasker in F.G. Smith's *Gospel Trumpet* "Editorial," to which we have already referred at length, was one of them. More on that subject later.

It is quite likely that others, as well, shared his views on several important issues–one of those views being the creeping "ecclesiasticism" taking over in Anderson. It appears from later events, I think, that a silent minority certainly existed "out there" in the hinterlands, waiting for the change in climate they hoped would eventually come. Few dared to be openly critical. The "influential brethren," after all, had the power of the *Gospel Trumpet* at their disposal–and it had already been used on quite a few occasions against others.

Brother Tasker attempted, then, to inform the "brethren" in North America concerning what had happened, as he saw it, by publishing all of the correspondence and documents he believed were pertinent to the case. He entitled the resulting 68-page "pamphlet" (as he calls it), *An Appeal to the Free and Autonomous Churches of*

*Christ in the Fellowship of the Evening Light.*

Apart from a two-page explanatory introduction, it was published without note or comment. (The notes and comments were to come much later in the margins of a copy Brother Tasker gave to a friend and supporter, Albert J. Kempin, and much later by Brother Kempin's widow to me.) This is based on the assumption that the evidence of wrongful dismissal was clear enough that readers could see it for themselves. It did not need to be pointed out to them. Brother Tasker was anxious that the churches, as "the ultimate earthly court of appeal," have "a chance to decide for themselves what seems to have been decided without them" (*An Appeal*, p. 2).

He confesses that when the Board's Resolution was made known to them, he had no thought of appealing to the churches in the Church of God fellowship. But, the Board informed them that "as far as the Board is concerned, no further difficulty exists between us and them, and that any difficulties that may exist now, exist between us and the church." Therefore, "it seems fitting that for us to communicate with the church in the only way open to us under the circumstances."

Brother Tasker was aware that some of his personal references to missionaries and Board members may have seemed a bit harsh at times. And that some of his remarks would likely be seen as "sharp." They are to be regretted now, he says, in view of their publication. "But they were not written for publication, and it must be remembered that when one is set for the defense of vital principles which he feels are in danger or thinks are being violated, he does not always stop to find soft words, but speaks straight out." Indeed! If you are Brother Tasker, that is. But this sharpness turned out to be costly indeed.

And so *An Appeal* was sent out, whether from Calcutta, where it was printed, or from North America, we have no way of knowing. Nor do we know how many were sent out. Brother F.G. Smith's *Gospel Trumpet* "Editorial" for January 22, 1925, says only that this "so-called 'appeal' has been quite widely distributed in America and elsewhere." [1] He continues with his rather strange logic, "*Any unbiased person* reading [this pamphlet] will have no difficulty in discerning the spirit that is prompting Brother Tasker's course" (italics mine, calling attention to the fact that Brother Smith was every bit as biased as Brother Tasker was–how could he not be under the circumstances, as President of the Missionary Board?).

## Financial Support

The stated purpose of the first pamphlet–and possibly even the second–is to appeal to the churches for financial support for the work the Taskers wanted to continue in India. Brother Tasker makes this appeal quite explicit. At first, he says, we had thought only of "writing to personal friends and other individuals who might wish to help continue the work we have been doing, in fellowship with the church in this country, among the crowds of Hindu and Mohammedan [Muslim] students of the Colleges here in Calcutta."

The final page of the pamphlet adds a P.S. "All donations should be sent to us direct by International P.O. Money Order, or by Dollar draft on New York, or by Sterling draft on London. Reports and financial statements will be sent to all supporters." It may be that a major

---

[1]  This Editorial refers also to a second "pamphlet," entitled *A Further Word to the Churches,* sent out little more than three weeks later by Brother Tasker. We have not been able to locate this. My curiosity is greatly aroused, but, I must confess, I do not know where or how even to begin searching for it since we appear not to have it in Church of God Archives. The Editorial also states that the Missionary Board "issued a pamphlet" which gives "a thorough explanation of the whole matter." This pamphlet was mailed out to "the ministers of the church in America whose names appear in the 1925 Year Book." We cannot locate this either. I doubt, however, that it would add much of anything new to the discussion. Brother Smith had, in editorials and other writings, fully expressed the "official" position as he saw it.

reason the Missionary Board sent out its own pamphlet was to plug what they saw as a possible hole in the financial dyke. Potentially, at least, they stood to lose quite a few dollars they could ill afford to lose—if indeed Brother Tasker was appealing to the Church of God generally (which I tend to doubt).

When I asked Mona Moors Tasker how the Taskers were supported after their separation from the Missionary Board, she replied that she really did not know anything too specific. "He never talked much about it," she said. But she went on to say, "I know he received donations from friends and from services rendered when called [by other churches in India]. He also had an investment in Montreal some relatives saved for him. They did not have an easy time during those days, but they lived simply and the Lord supplied all their needs in various ways."

Some of the "services rendered" that Sister Moors Tasker knew of were: frequent preaching at the Methodist Episcopal Church in Calcutta, "when he was there;" and teaching classes and other work at the Y.M.C.A. Apparently, he had many associations with other evangelical Protestant groups in India and traveled quite extensively, often receiving some small remuneration for his services.

### *"The Free and Autonomous Churches of Christ"*

I must confess to being greatly intrigued—which may tempt me to make too much of it—by the full title of *An Appeal*: "An Appeal to the Free and Autonomous Churches of Christ in the Fellowship of the Evening Light." Was this simply Brother Tasker's way of appealing to Church of God congregations in North America who were uneasy—and perhaps on the fence—over the "organizational revolution" taking place in Anderson?

Or was it an appeal to congregations of the Church of God that had already decided on which side of the fence they stood? Brother Smith's Editorial says only that *An Appeal* had been "quite widely distributed in America and elsewhere," with the "elsewhere" referring, perhaps, to Canada—and perhaps to individual missionaries being sponsored by the Church of God (Anderson, Indiana).

It is likely then that Harry Nelson, one of Brother Tasker's long-time friends and associates in Ontario, would have received *An Appeal* and responded to it. Brother Nelson was greatly instrumental in establishing the work of the Church of God in Ontario and he and his wife were faithful supporters of both Brother and Sister Tasker and Sister Josephine McCrie as missionaries.

By the time *An Appeal* was written, Harry Nelson had long been "on the outs" with both the Church of God in Ontario and the Anderson brethren (he did not accept the then-reigning Church of God version of the doctrine of sanctification). In 1911, the "tongues movement" began disrupting the Church of God in Ontario, resulting in division and the loss of several Church of God congregations. Apparently, Nelson was godly, spiritual, and genuinely humble, a man of "marked ability and a pleasing personality" (Beverley C. Anderson, *A History of the Church of God in Ontario 1882-1955*, p. 75f).

Nelson was a close personal friend of Brother Tasker and, in spite of all the "tongues movement" controversy swirling around him,[2] Brother Tasker insisted that "Harry never went with the Pentecostal movement but to the end of his days sought to hold with the Church of God movement" (Anderson, p.73). It is quite possible, then, that Nelson and some of his associates in Ontario represent at least some part of "the free and autonomous churches of Christ in the fellowship of the evening light." This is largely speculation. But, in view of Brother Tasker's long and close association with Nelson and the churches in Ontario, it makes a great deal of sense.

---

[2] Brother Tasker agreed with Nelson on sanctification, but did not agree with the "tongues movement" and, in fact, wrote against it. His association with Nelson, however, convinced him that Nelson had experienced a "genuine gift of tongues" (as a prayer language). He writes, in a personal letter to Beverley Anderson, February 1955, "Smith and Reardon both accepted Harry's experience as genuine, the former even saying to me, after we had heard Harry pray and sing in "tongues," "Bro. Tasker, we just <u>have</u> to get more of the Holy Spirit in our work or we will have more of <u>man</u>" (Anderson, pp. 75-76).

A much more certain source of financial and moral support for the Taskers was Fred Bruffett and his associates in the American Conference of Undenominational Churches, of which Bruffett was Vice-President (another former Church of God pastor, T.E. Howard, was president). He was also Editor of the Prayer and Answer Department of the *Christian Advocate*. He seems also to have published his own paper–so Brother Smith indicates in his January 22, 1925 editorial–entitled, "The Pioneer of A New Era." [3]

The *Pioneer* article that caused Brother Smith to turn all of his guns on Bruffett (who earlier had been nominated by the Missionary Board to fill one of its vacancies–but was not elected), attacked the Church of God for its "creeping ecclesiasticism." He objected to the Ministerial Assembly and the various boards being set up to "centralize" the work of the Church.

This trend to "man-rule" is, Bruffet says in another publication, an obvious betrayal of the reformation principles on which the Church of God was founded. He writes: "I spent nearly eighteen years with the *Gospel Trumpet* . . .and I don't think there is another body of people in existence that is trying harder to sectarianize the name of the church than they, except it be the Church of Christ" (*Pioneer*, June 1926). This, indeed, sounds very much like Brother Tasker. Not as smooth and polished, but like him all the same.

In the *Pioneer* of December, 1925, Bruffett defends his congregation against "reports circulated at [the] last convention at Anderson" that the Lincoln (Nebraska?) church was "on the rocks and about to be sold for indebtedness."

---

[3] This and the following information comes from the Frederick George Smith Papers, housed in Church of God Archives. In the file containing information concerning Fred Bruffett is a list of names from the *Pioneer* of "rejected ministers taken into fellowship." They are as follows: T.E. Howard, Mr. and Mrs. W.J. Henry, George L. Cole, Harry W. Nelson, L.H. Morgan, A.B. Stanberry, Guy Little, Mr. and Mrs. G.P. Tasker, Nathan C. McNeill, L.V. Strickland, Josephine McCrie, Mr. and Mrs. H.A. Brooks, George Bailey, Paul J. Kenagy, H.B. Centz, S.L. Johnson, Charles E. Driver, and J.E. Forrest.

Not so, he says. "It is both successful and prosperous." "Ram-rods" from Anderson "headquarters" had "tried to wreck it a few years ago," but they had failed, suffering "a stinging defeat." Since they "declared their freedom," the Lincoln church had prospered in every way. He continues:

> Eight preachers have been ordained through the church in the last few years. Many have been converted and healed. . . .All glory to Christ, the great head of the church.
> Three missionaries are off for the field shortly. Miss Josephine McCrie sails in September, and Mr. and Mrs. G.P. Tasker sail a few months later, all to India. . . . It might be interesting to state here that the Taskers formerly worked under the Gospel Trumpet Company Missionary Board, but were rudely dismissed and forced to come home at their own expense because they desire to cooperate with other Christian missionaries on the field and put over a united program, the only kind that can possibly be put over successfully on the foreign fields.

Apparently Sister Mona Moors Tasker knew nothing of this association, or had forgotten about it. (It probably was not a long-term arrangement in any event.) At the time, however, she was in India working with the Church of God at the Shelter in Cuttack, in the eastern state of Orissa. She would not have had much contact with the Taskers during those years. She had arrived in India only in 1922 and, at 25, was much too young to have been a confidante of the Taskers, then in their mid-fifties.

In any event, the information from Fred Bruffett's writings clarifies very considerably how the Taskers were maintained in India as independent missionaries—at least in the beginning of their independent years, although probably not for the whole period. And we also know who at least some of the "free and autonomous churches of Christ in the fellowship of the evening light" most likely were. The data, I think, support such inferences.

## *Bangalore*

The Taskers remained in Calcutta until April 1925, when they sailed from Bombay to Montreal at their own expense. Undoubtedly, they returned to North America to raise money to support themselves and their missionary work. They returned to Calcutta in May, 1927. (This and other chronological information has been supplied by David Davis from Brother Tasker's own writing in his wife Minnie's Bible of which I spoke earlier.)

They began their work as independent missionaries in Calcutta, opening a Reading Room on Garpar Road in July, 1927. They continued this work until March, 1933. At that point, they sailed to Lebanon (then Syria), "to teach in Atchinak's school in Beirut." [4] The next note by Brother Tasker indicates that they sailed a year later from Beirut, arriving in New York in April, 1934 for a brief furlough—probably relating to financial support. They sailed again for India in December that same year, arriving in Bangalore,

---

[4] This is a reference to Vartan Atchinak. Dr. Kenneth Crose, youngest son of John D. and Pearl Crose—and one of the very influential professors in my life at Pacific Bible College (now Warner Pacific College)— grew up in Beirut and later returned there as a Church of God missionary. He knew Atchinak and, as a high school senior, well remembers the Taskers, who spent considerable time in the Crose home. For further information, he directed me to Lester Crose's book, *Passport for a Reformation,* pp. 34 and 42. Early in the 1900s, Atchinak, an independent evangelical minister, had started the Bible Lands Gospel Mission. In 1907, he happened to meet Brothers Tasker, Reardon, and Brooks in Cairo. He requested teachers for his school (apparently a church-sponsored public school). It seems that in 1934 John D. Crose recommended Brother Tasker as a teacher in the school. The Taskers were leaving Calcutta at that point—perhaps due primarily to Sister Tasker's failing health—and needed work. During his time there, Brother Tasker learned some Arabic (languages came quite easily to him). One evening in the Tasker's apartment, I recall listening to a discourse by him on Islam. To demonstrate a point, he got out a Muslim prayer rug, knelt on it, and with his forehead touching the floor, recited the Muslim *shahadah*, or confession of faith, in fluent Arabic.

South India in February, 1935. (Brother Tasker notes that Minnie suffered increasing nervous illness" during the return trip to India.)

In Bangalore, Brother Tasker served as pastor of the Union Christian Church–how long is not clear (he does not give dates and places for the years 1935-1946, other than noting, "Then over to Richmond Town, then Ulsoor Road") but it may have been for quite a number of years. This church, so Mona Moors Tasker says, was "for everyone," missionaries, Anglo-Indians, and Indians. He preached, taught Bible classes, and did "a lot of writing."

In January, 1944, he became pastor of the Methodist Church in Bangalore. In the Tasker papers that I and others have collected is a small hand-bound volume entitled "Bulletin Meditations." These cover "the entire period of my pastorate in the Methodist Church in Richmond Town, Bangalore, Jan 1, 1944 to Mar 1946." These bulletin meditations were basically sermonettes. So, it seems, he had more than enough to keep him well occupied through the war years until his final return to Canada in 1946.[5]

The move to Bangalore was probably necessitated by the almost total breakdown in Sister Minnie Tasker's health. Undoubtedly, the worry and stress engendered by the Painful Separation played a quite major role in this. Then, we must not overlook the sense of alienation she must have felt from people she loved deeply. Such emotional and psychological stress can be difficult to deal with at the best of times, but when thousands of miles from one's homeland and family, it can be devastating.

---

[5] From a personal visit by Borman Roy Sohkhia, an outstanding Church of God leader in Meghalaya, India, I have just recently learned that Brother Tasker was instrumental in founding a "union" Bible school in Bangalore. This school, he said, may have been the seed idea that eventually led to the outstanding interdenominational Union Theological College. While writing his book—now at the printers—on the history of the Church of God in India, Brother Sohkhia concluded that Brother Tasker was one of the most important figures in the history of the Church of God in India. He was a great man and a great scholar, beloved in Meghalaya, and mightily used of God throughout India.

But the dismal environment of Calcutta, with its heat, noise, and grime, packed as it was with hundreds of thousands of the desperately poor, was a problem all on its own. In a personal letter to a friend (and supporter?) in California, Brother Tasker notes that Minnie had been unable "for quite a few months" to keep up her correspondence. "No more trouble in the chest, but anaemic, upset in the digestive tract, and distressed . . . in her nerves."

Sister Tasker's illness—including long periods of depression—appears to have intensified in the last five years of her life. It was very hard on both of them. Gradually, she lost interest in all of those things in which she had been so interested and involved, but nearly to the end retained a keen interest in her husband's work. Following her "merciful" death on November 10, 1940, Brother Tasker wrote a long letter on November 11 (which is incorrectly dated 1941) to "my Min's" family, the Criswells, concerning her final months and hours. In it, he describes how much her support and counsel had meant to him through the long years of their ministry:

> When I would read to her from books along spiritual lines or talk over my sermons with her or read them and my articles to her, she was as understanding as ever she was and as able as ever to give her always invaluable counsel and criticism, and what I personally owe to her on this and other lines I shall never be able adequately to express. In fact I thought she became better and better as a counsellor as her mind and spirit ripened in the fire of the discipline through which she herself was passing. She was certainly God's gift to me, and with all my heart I have ever thanked Him for her and all her wise and loving counsel.

In his interview, R.R. Byrum had this to say of Minnie Criswell Tasker: "She died rejected by her friends, the church she had so faithfully served, forgotten by friends for whom she had so earnestly prayed. What an end to a beautiful, dedicated life. Let's never let it happen again that personal ambition should run so wild. Let it not happen again in our fellowship!" All I can say is "Amen!"

In 1941, Brother Tasker wrote to his fellow missionary, Josephine McCrie, who was working in Calcutta also as an independent missionary, and proposed marriage. She readily agreed and they were married in Bangalore. They continued to serve there until after World War II had ended. Brother Tasker was, by then, 74 years of age and had served continuously in India for 34 years, Sister Josephine for 42.

### And Canada

Since Sister Josephine Tasker was a Canadian, the Taskers agreed to retire in Canada. His good friend, Leonard E. Millensifer, a pioneer minister of the Church of God in Western Canada, persuaded him to settle in the region of Penticton, British Columbia where there was a Church of God congregation at Trout Creek (Summerland) in need of support and encouragement. And so our story comes full circle, for it was here that I met the Taskers.

Josephine McCrie Tasker was the Sister Tasker I knew in Penticton—and what an unusual person she was.[6] She died in 1954, and the following year, Brother Tasker was married to Mona Moors, who had been a missionary of the Church of God at the Shelter in Cuttack, India from 1922 to 1955. She was 55 years of age, he 80. (For someone who a Board member or two thought could not get along with his fellow missionaries, he seemed to do quite well!)

After his marriage to Mona Moors in 1955, Brother Tasker was offered the position of chaplain in a newly-built

---

[6] Brother Tasker never owned a motor car, so he and Sister Tasker rode the several miles from Penticton to church with a friend and me. We talked and laughed a good deal. Both of the Taskers had a droll sense of humor. On one occasion, we were discussing the wearing of jewelry—and in particular, a young woman in the church who wore a gold cross on a gold chain. Brother Tasker saw nothing at all wrong with the practice, but Sister Josephine was not quite so sure. She assured us she herself would not want to wear such a thing, but would never judge anyone who did. "Anyway," she said, laughing, "I always thought we were to *bear* the cross, not *wear* it!"

"retirement" center (Valley View Lodge) on a hill over-looking  beautiful Lake Okanagan. It was there, three years later, he died–possibly from pneumonia and other complications from a fall that had broken his hip and confined him to bed for the last few months of his life.

## Regret and Reconciliation

Now it's time to circle back again–this time to 1936. This, I suppose, is "the rest of the story." Some of it, at any rate. In that year, the Missionary Board passed another Resolution, this time expressing regret for the events of 1924 and expressing the hope that if God so leads, "actual working relations" might be resumed. How did this come about? Why this *volte-face*?

### Letter of Apology

Toward the end of June, 1935, Brother Tasker wrote a letter to E.A. Reardon, long-time member of the Missionary Board, apologizing for his sharp and aggressive letters in 1923 and 1924. In disposing of a box of old correspondence which he had kept since the Calcutta days, he came across copies of his letters to the Board. "As I read over those old letters," he says, "in the calm and detached atmosphere of the present time, I found myself becoming impressed with something, that, in the heat of the earlier time, had . . . quite escaped me."

And what was that? " In my paraphrase: "That I had never seen things from your point of view, or realized how much you had to bear. But now that I can see the whole thing from a new angle, and I fully realize how much forbearance you showed." In his own words:

> I now feel that instead of censuring you so much I sympathize with you in your difficulty and am only sorry that being so full of my own matter I was unable to or did not feel that sympathy in those days, when doubtless such a feeling on my part, deep and sincere, might have enabled me to do still more than I did to prevent if possible the final

breach. But things conscientiously felt to be more vital than any other considerations predominantly occupied [my] mind, and it is all past now. But you know that I love you, hold nothing against you in my heart, feel a deep sympathy for your problem, and desire only your prayers and fellowship in the eternal, spiritual bonds that are in Christ Jesus our Lord (*from a copy of the letter given to me by John D. Crose*).

It seems that Brother Reardon may have responded to Brother Tasker, asking permission to read this letter to the Missionary Board in annual session—and that Brother Tasker must have agreed. Thus in the Annual Meeting of the Missionary Board in June, 1936, the letter was duly presented. In view of this letter, the Minutes state, "it was moved by C.J. Blewitt and seconded by C.E. Byers" that the Resolutions Committee draw up a Resolution responding to Brother Tasker.

### The Resolution

This Resolution was quickly prepared and presented to the Board later the same day. Apparently it took only a small fraction of the time to write than was taken by the 1924 Resolution. Here it is, beginning with the second "whereas:"

WHEREAS, In said letter Brother Tasker, refering to past events which led to the rupture of his working relations with the Board, now expresses particular regrets because of his part in the affair, and according to our understanding of said letter to Brother Reardon, wishes to assure us of his sympathetic, brotherly attitude toward us all; therefore be it

RESOLVED, That we as a Board convey to Brother Tasker our deep appreciation of this letter and the spirit that prompted it; and, further that we wish to express ourselves definitely on the following points:

1. That while during the period of controversy with him we tried to act conscientiously, in accordance with what concept of duty at the time seemed to require, we do not wish to assume that our methods of procedure were in all respects without real faults. To whatever extent these shortcomings of ours–whether individual or official– hindered better understanding or reconciliation, we hereby express our deep regrets.

2. There is no doubt that time itself, and additional experience, have modified some of our own attitudes, in certain respects, while we believe and feel that we are still loyal to God and to his cause. In other words, some of the very things that occasioned much of the controversy have themselves been largely dissolved.

3. We wish nothing but the most brotherly relations with Brother and Sister Tasker. We pray God to bless, direct, and use them. And if God, in his plan, so leads that, eventually, there may be a resumption of actual working relations, we see no reason, as far as our attitude is concerned, why such might not result   (Missionary Board Minutes, June 10, 1936).

The Board requested the Secretary-Treasurer, Adam W. Miller, to give a copy of the letter to Brother Reardon, who was to forward it to Brother and Sister Tasker with a covering letter. The Secretary-Treasurer was also instructed to write to Brother Tasker, requesting permission to send the Resolution, together with a copy of his June, 1935 letter to all Church of God missionaries in India. Brother Tasker not only agreed, but asked that copies be sent to the missionaries in China and to Brother and Sister John D. Crose. The adoption of the Resolution was moved by F.G. Smith and seconded by E.A. Reardon.

In view of the fact that Brother Tasker was only about a year away from the Missionary Board's mandatory retirement age–and the Board did not allow retirement on the field--he apparently made no attempt to be reinstated as a Church of God missionary. Besides, his wife's health was failing rapidly and reinstatement would probably have meant a move back to North India. At that point it seemed out of the question. But he rejoiced at the reconciliation, nonetheless. He had at last accepted his own part in the whole affair and that gave him a great sense of release.

## A Change Of Heart

In 1936, the Missionary Board consisted of 15 members: C.E. Brown, President; E.A. Reardon, Vice-President; Adam W. Miller, Secretary-Treasurer, A.F. Gray, E.E. Byrum, F.G. Smith, C.J. Blewitt, Axchie Bolitho, Ida Rowe, Nora Hunter, J.W. Phelps, S.J. Taylor, H.M. Riggle, R.L. Berry, and C.E. Byers. Eight of these had been on the Missionary Board in 1924. Only one of that Board had voted against that Resolution. This new Resolution passed without a single dissenting vote. What had changed?

Brother Tasker certainly had not changed his theological views. Nor had he changed his mind on organizational matters, such as the appointment of field secretaries, or the imposition of foreign structures on national churches. His attitude toward the Missionary Board had certainly changed. The further he got from the time of the Painful Separation, the more he realized that, under the circumstances, the Board could do little else than dismiss him.

But his own change of heart cannot, by itself, explain the Missionary Board's change of heart—even to the extent of suggesting that reinstatement was not out of the question. His most vigorous early antagonists, F.G. Smith, E.E. Byrum, C.E. Brown, R.L. Berry, C.J.Blewitt, and J.W. Phelps were still on the Board in 1936. To be sure, they were a minority on this Board, but we must not miss the fact that F.G. Smith, for one, played a prominent role in getting the Resolution written and passed.

The whole process seemed to take very little time, compared to the many hours spent in 1924. It was as if the Board—and particularly some of those who had been on the Board in 1924–were eager and anxious to make amends and to heal this open wound. Perhaps many of them had come to realize that Brother Tasker had been right in many respects, after all. Brother Phelps later said, "Brother Tasker was 95% right." To which Brother Tasker responded, "Poor Phelps!" (Does that suggest, by the way, that the 1924 Board was 95% wrong? Apparently Brother Phelps thought so at that point.) As Brother John D. Crose said, "Brother Tasker was right; he was just right at the wrong time time"–and perhaps in the wrong way. I think I've heard that before from others.

In his hand-written notations and additions in my copy of *An Appeal,* Brother Tasker writes that in 1924 the Board had his name removed from the Church of God Year Book. Five members, he says, "lived to acknowledge this mistake and offer personal apologies." They were: Berry; Brown; Phelps; Sanders; and Bessie Byrum. However, in 1947, in spite of appeals by John D. Crose and H.C. Heffren, the Board refused to rescind this action. He concludes: "Time and grace can heal spiritual wounds, but can never restore a severed official connection."

While I was puzzling over the Missionary Board's change of heart and their eagerness to pass the second Resolution, I went through Brother Tasker's 1923-1924 correspondence with the Board again. This time, I found a letter written in 1923 by Brother Tasker that suggested at least one of the reasons for this "dignified haste." Here's what I found.

On October 8, 1923, Brother Tasker addressed a "letter of surrender," so to speak, to the Missionary Board. Apparently, both Brother Smith and Brother Reardon had written to him personally and had visited him in India in 1921. Brother Reardon, particularly, had pointed out that he had been too militant and "caustic" in many of his criticisms, making him appear like "an outsider." Brother Tasker admitted that Brother Reardon was right and said, "I regret this very much." He goes on, "I certainly did not mean to appear estranged, for I know I am not. Practically my whole Christian life has been given to the work of the reformation, every earthly prospect having long ago been sacrificed for it. Shall I then turn away from it because of any faults and dangers . . .? I think not. I have too many faults of my own." He writes:

> I cannot ask forgiveness for my zeal in the interests of sound doctrine and the elimination of ideas that I believe are subversive of the movement's non-sectarian and spiritual character as a restoration of pure Christianity; but it is surely a very serious defect in any teacher for him to be so full of the thought of pointing out something that he overlooks the necessity of expressing himself in acceptable terms. Please, my brethren, forgive me this, and also please pray the Lord to reveal to me anything else you may think is amiss in me. . . .
>
> As for myself therefore I will submit to any points of controversy; for, after all, these are only matters of *our developing understanding*; but I can find no way to consent to separation or dissociation from you, for that is a matter touching the heart and soul and would violate something I regard as sacred and absolutely vital and fundamental (*An Appeal,* p.46-47, italics mine).

In another handwritten notation at the top of my copy of *An Appeal*, he adds this information: "On writing the following letter, I read it to J.J.M. Nichols Roy, who happened to be in Calcutta at the time. He said, 'Brother Tasker, the brethren will take no action against you when they read that letter.'" But they did, much to his dismay and bewilderment. The letter, he said, was not acknowledged.

Brother Tasker learned several years later, so he writes, that "the Board as such never saw the letter. Smith and Phelps (?) suppressed it. Riggle assured me that if he had seen that letter, he would never have voted as he did." He adds in parentheses, "F.G. Smith acknowledged before me that it had been received. But it seems to have been deliberately withheld from the Board."

Had members of the 1924 Board later learned of it and thus their change of heart? I think little of most conspiracy theories, but was this a conspiracy to silence a critic who was hitting too close to home? Was it a desperate attempt to save a rapidly sinking budget? Only they knew for sure, I guess. We probably can't know the answer to these questions conclusively at this point.

## A Changing Climate

Isn't it amazing how much our *view* of events changes as our *position* relative to them changes? Sometimes our habits of thought and self-awareness gradually move us to a new point of view, often so slowly we are not aware we're even moving—as happened with Brother Tasker. Other times, the shift is more sudden, cataclysmic.

This, I think happened to Brother Smith and some of those closest to him. The Church of God as a whole had changed considerably since the establishment of the General Ministerial Assembly in 1917. By 1930, even some of the "old guard," who were largely unaware of how much it had changed, were forced to take notice. They themselves began to change with the times. Some, of course, were more comfortable being behind the times and so stayed there playing on their one-stringed harps.

A number of cataclysmic events signaled the extent of the changes going on through the 1920s. In 1930, by action of the Gospel Trumpet Board, F.G. Smith was removed as Editor-in-Chief. When the Gospel Trumpet Board brought forward the name of H.M. Riggle, the Ministerial Assembly refused to ratify him (perhaps one of the very few times, if not the only time, in the history of the Assembly this has happened). Subsequently, Charles E. Brown was accepted.

Why this refusal? Was Brother Riggle too closely tied with Brothers Smith and Byrum—who, like Smith, had also been forced to vacate the Editor's Chair? Did the Assembly fear a continuation of what many saw as autocratic and centralized rule? Did they want to limit the teaching authority and ecclesiastical power of the Editor-in-Chief? It seems so. (Doubtless, the situation was much more complex than that. Few things are nearly so simple and straighforward as they seem on the surface.)

It is possible to conclude, I think, that the mood of the Assembly had shifted considerably—however complex the reasons. Perhaps they wanted no more of oligarchy, that is, the near-absolute rule by an elite few, which had increasingly characterized the Church of God over the years. Democracy was in, and theocracy as it had been practiced was out. In any event, as the years went by after 1917, they increasingly flexed their new-found muscles.

Sometime—probably before 1930 (the oral record is not clear)—Brother Smith brought a Resolution to the Ministerial Assembly asking that they declare Gospel Trumpet literature (that is, doctrinal books and pamphlets) published before 1924 to be "the standard literature of the Church of God" (he probably would have added "reformation movement"). He was soundly rebuffed by the Assembly. The next day, a motion to strike the Minute from the record was made and overwhelmingly passed. Thus, it does not appear in official Ministerial Assembly Minutes. (I am aware, of course, that this is not documented. It was told to me by John W.V. Smith, who said he got the information from several who were there and participated in the event.)

I recount this story–which I can find no good reason not to believe–not just because it probably happened and I think it's the job of historians to do that, but because it so well illustrates my argument that the leadership of the Church of God was quite rapidly shifting ground. What was causing that, I will leave to our professional historians to decide. The events of 1930-1931 suggest that something momentous had been going on throughout the 1920s—but undoubtedly had begun earlier than that.

This is true as well of the dismissal of Brother Tasker. Whether conspiracy or not–and conspiracy may be too strong a term–it did not happen "in a corner." It exercised the minds and spirits of many–due as much to Brother Smith's Editorial of January 22, 1925 as anything else. A perhaps surprisingly large minority, but still only a minority, had not, in the words of some of them, "bowed the knee to geographical comeoutism" or to an exclusivist view of the Church or its place in the Kingdom.

One of the minority voices was that of Brother E.A. Reardon. Even from the beginning, he supported Brother Tasker. He was influential and packed a lot of clout on both sides of the "house." As early as 1915, he obliquely expressed doubts of the prevailing theology and system:

> Those who come out of Babylon under a harsh preacher are frequently born of a wrong spirit, and if a dozen of them do see the evils of sectarianism, they can scarcely keep from judging and criticizing one another. They are a very hard lot to get lined up for the Lord. They are a poor example of a flock which is supposed to be better than a sect. They will likely worship the reformation instead of the Lord, and with their sectarian spirit, they will hold the reformation in exactly the same way that the sectarian holds his sect, and be more loyal to it than to God and his church. . . . Some never seem to be in their element unless they are threshing Babylon, exposing false teachers, or clubbing wolves. Such preachers rarely give the sheep a good meal (*Our Ministerial Letter: A Message to Young Ministers,* Vol II, No. 10, pp 8-9).

Brother Reardon soon became "the point man" for those who wanted change, but who, like Brother Tasker, wanted to remain part of the Church of God. In 1929, he was asked to give the opening address to the Ministerial Assembly. He decided to lay it on the line. His address was almost pure "Tasker." He was, of course, neither copying him nor apeing him—although it is not likely that he would have been unaware of Brother Tasker's positions even then—but simply stating his own deep and studied convictions that had probably begun to form long before 1924. Among other things, he said:

> There is no one place on earth from which God is directing all his Kingdom and his salvation work. There is no one body of people on earth who can claim an exclusive right to Christ and to all his light and truth. . . . I cannot conceive of [Christ] as confining his operations exclusively to this movement, and I am quite sure that the representative minds and spiritual hearts of our people do not hold such

a view. . . . Christ would certainly ignore our reformation exclusiveness and cultivate, first of all, that
unity that is in himself. . . . The expectation that all
sheep of the Lord are eventually coming to us as a
movement is not at all necessary to the success of
God's plan. Anyhow, this movement is only one
phase of the great reformation work that God is
doing among his people in the world. It is true that
this reformation is a concrete expression of the
working of God's Spirit in the Christian world, and it
has its place, but it is not all there is of God's
reformation work" (from Barry Callen, *Following the
Light,* "The Problems of Christian Unity," pp. 134-
135).

And there was much more in the same vein. "We are
missing much," he said, "because we have cut ourselves
off from association and fellowship with other Christian
people who in many respects could enrich us." He also
spoke of those "among us" who could do much more for
Christ and his reformation "if they were not confined and
hobbled by a critical and narrow spirit in our own work."
The furor was immediate and intense—so John A.
Morrison reports in *As the River Flows.* He writes: "As
Reardon read his paper, the atmosphere in the Assembly
grew tense. Clouds of fear and concern covered the faces
of many brethren. When the session broke up they
gathered in clusters all over the grounds and talked with
many gestures" (p. 169).
The majority of the Assembly clearly did not like what
they had heard from Brother Reardon and retaliated by
voting him out of all Assembly offices—except the
Missionary Board, strangely enough. He was reelected to
the Board a few days later, receiving nearly twice as many
votes as his "opponent." He was reelected again, with an
even larger majority in 1934 and in 1936 was elected Vice-
President of the Board.
Clearly, I think, a revolution was in the making. Comeoutism was gradually losing its grip on the minds of many
in the Church of God. A broader vision of the church was
infiltrating the collective consciousness of ministers and lay

persons alike—however slowly in some cases. To be sure, the old vision stubbornly held its ground in many areas–as it does in several revised forms yet today–and continued for many years to represent the view of the majority. (Possibly because the majority were concentrated in the eastern half of the United States, which had been the geographical center of comeoutism. The Midwest and South may have been more heavily influenced by "come-out" views than other regions were.)

But in high places, things were changing. Persons like Brother Reardon–and he certainly was not alone or he would not have so well survived the Ministerial Assembly of 1929–continued to exercise considerable influence. Perhaps he was ahead of his times—and he certainly believed he was part of a much larger company—but not too far ahead as Brother Tasker appears to have been.

By the 1930s, the Church of God, in many respects, was beginning to catch up with Brother Tasker. So much so that the Missionary Board had little hesitation in suggesting re-association. This would be incomprehensible if we were to conclude that the "revolution" between 1924 and 1936 began only in 1924, as a result of the Tasker debacle, or in 1929, as a result of Brother Reardon's speech. Of course, for some of the Missionary Board members—those who had been on the 1924 Board—the fact of the withheld letter may have weighed more heavily than any major broadening of vision on their part. But the vision of the majority of the Board seems unquestionably to have broadened. Comeoutism simply could not survive for long in this changing climate.

What it suggests, I think, is that Brother Tasker was anything but alone in at least some of his theological views. Evidently, he had begun to express these views publicly in America, even before 1918, the point at which the Missionary Board began to insist that he return home on furlough to discuss these very disconcerting and "liberal" doctrinal ideas. Those views were probably, as he himself said, well known to the "influential brethren" of the Church long before 1924 and some, at least, agreed with him. Thus his bewilderment at why they should suddenly become such an issue in 1924.

## Conclusion

So where did it all end? In reality, it never did. It's still going on. Brother Tasker is only a historical memory–and I hope now a good memory for more than just the few of us left who knew him for the great man he was. But what he represents in our history has no ending. The majority of the Church came eventually to agree with Brother Phelps that Brother Tasker was "95% right."

The vast majority of the Church now has little allegiance to–and for most, probably no historical memory of–the "geographical comeoutism" of our pioneers. Some simply push it aside as a period piece of interest only to historians and antiquarians. When I came on the scene in Western Canada in the late 1940s, the concept did not appear to be anywhere around. I can't remember hearing a sermon, lecture, or conversation on the subject.

At Alberta Bible Institute (now Gardner College), what we were taught about the church agreed in the main with Brother Tasker's view. (Brother Tasker was very well accepted at ABI and in local congregations in Western Canada in those days.) Even his views on sanctification, which earlier had caused some fuss among the "influential brethren" in Anderson, did not generally cause any churchly panic that I can recall. He was a respected and honored man among us.

By the 1950s, things had moved a long way from the blinkered view of the church that had prevailed a generation earlier. Many of us were listening to the Christian Brotherhood Hour with W. Dale Oldham at the helm. In copying one of those programs to audio cassette tape for someone a few days ago, I was struck by a statement at the beginning of the program: "The Christian Brotherhood Hour calls Christians everywhere to work together toward a united church for a divided world." Precisely what Brother Tasker and Brother Reardon had been saying in the 1920s. In our case, that stream of thinking in the Church certainly held the field.

My heritage, then, was that which taught that the Church of God was a "family" of Christian believers among other "families" of Christian believers. Those in a "family" cannot reasonably believe that their way of being "family" is the only possible way. Nor can it be held to be true—as have those who have insisted that the Church of God alone comprises the church of God—that if a family is not unique, doing what no other family on earth is doing, then it has no reason for existence.

The human family is made up of many, many extended families, each with its own special genius. To say that the part has no reason for existence other than to be the whole is absurd. Of course, we can go back to thinking so if we choose—and some have—but I've never yet found a comfortable personal spiritual or intellectual fetal position. That is simply not my Church of God heritage. Brother Tasker and a host of others saw to that.

I am thankful for my "family" heritage. It has helped determine and shape who I am spiritually. That "family" is important to me, no matter how it came into existence. It does not need to be peculiar or unique to have a reason for being.[7] It holds much in common with other "families" as well as much that is particular to itself. It is one—and only one—of the many "families" that make up the great People of God. It looks a great deal like many other families, but it is special to me. I am not at all bothered by the realization that it has no claim on the "front seat." But, then, neither does any other "family." In God's Kingdom, the front seat is occupied only by Christ—and all the rest of us are merely brothers and sisters.

That much I learned from one of the giants of our history. The forty or more years since then have convinced me that he stood taller and saw farther than most of his generation in the Church of God. That so few of us have been able to benefit from that is one of the abiding ironies of our collective history.

---

[7] "We have exactly the same 'excuse' or reason for existing as a separate or distinct group that any other group of Christian believers has, no more and no less. In short, we have no unique reason for our existence. We exist for the same reason that the first Christians existed, to glorify God and serve Christ with the rest of His 'body'" (One of Brother Tasker's marginal jottings.)

## Chapter 6

## WHERE DOES ALL OF THIS LEAD?

We have considered Brother Tasker's story in rather great detail. But, as I said in the beginning, the story is multi-threaded and complex. Without more detail than may be considered usual for such biographies, however, that complexity would be missed and important connections to the larger history of the Church of God overlooked.

Brother Tasker's story is interwoven with many other stories. To understand him more completely, that interweaving must be recognized and made sense of. This is what I mean by context. Stories, then, make sense only in the context of many other stories. That we can never get to the end of this interweaving should not deter us from making rigorous attempts to do so. Better to do it incompletely (and, in some sense, all attempts must be incomplete) than to write a story as if it were the only one that happened. We've all read at least one of those stories. They leave us with many questions and very few answers.

But having told the story as completely as our sources will allow, I am loathe to leave it there without attempting to connect it to my ecclesiastical world. I'm not committed to the notion that a story, to be a really good story, must have a moral. Sometimes a story is a "good" story simply because it informs and inspires us, leaving us bigger and better people than we were–more whole, more sensitive and caring, more aware of who we ourselves are.

All the same, since I, at least, have gotten considerably more than just a glimpse at where I've been, I would like to relate that to where I'm going–particularly in my own thinking about this "family" of which I consider myself very much a part. What does this heavily-intertwined story of Brother Tasker mean to me? What kinds of questions do I see it raising that I want to reflect upon? I'm not at all sure where this will lead–but, then, I tend to write like that anyway, never quite sure where I'll come out. So on to the top of the hill to find out what's on the other side.

## Alternative Visions

One of the things we've seen in this story is the painful clash of alternative visions of what the Church of God is and what it should be about. Brother Smith–whose "apostolic succession" seemed unassailable–and the "influential brethren" gathered around him (Byrum; Byers; Riggle; Brown; Berry; and Phelps), supported by the vast majority of the Church, vigorously defended their passionate conviction that the Church of God (Anderson) was the church of God of the New Testament. Indeed, they insisted, it was prophesied in Scripture–appearing right on schedule, just as Brother Warner figured it would and Brother Smith and company believed it had. This is not to say that some did not modify their position over time. Brother Riggle seems to have done so, as his articles in the *Gospel Trumpet*, Jan. 1925 certainly suggest.

Brother Tasker, Brother Khan, Brother Nichols Roy, Brother Reardon, Brother Teasley and many others (how many we don't know, since those in power wrote most of the history–but probably more than we realize) saw things very differently. They were convinced that the only way you could "find" the Church of God in so-called prophetic texts–which they believed were peripheral texts read out of context–was to put it there in the first place. Then it could be quite easily "found." For them, the Church of God was a particular expression of the biblical church of God. That church, which had many particular expressions, consisted of all who were true, sanctified believers in Christ, no matter to what Church they belonged.

Thus, when Brother Smith and the majority around him "saw" the church of God, they saw something quite different than Brother Tasker and his colleagues and supporters "saw." They had two differing visions of the same reality, visions that clashed. The result was tragic for Brothers Tasker, Khan, and Nichols Roy, at least. (If Fred Bruffet is to be believed, a number of other well-known persons became dissociated as well.)

## The Question

And, thus, my question. Can a Church such as the Church of God (Anderson) tolerate alternative visions? It certainly appears not to have done so in its first fifty years. Its record in the next fifty years was considerably better, but not unblemished. In that period, the majority of the first fifty years gradually became the minority. They did not, to be sure, accept their minority status and in true minority fashion fought against the ideology of the new majority, asserting by every means possible that they were the "true church of God." Only by following their vision, so they insisted—and continue to insist—could God's true and only reformation be gotten back on track.

One has only to think of our friends in Christ at Guthrie, Oklahoma and Newark, Ohio who have "come out" of the Church of God (Anderson, Indiana). Each of these has its spin-offs, one of them actually publishing the *Gospel Trumpet*, its masthead identical in every detail to the masthead of the earliest *Gospel Trumpets* published by Brother Warner and the Fishers. The Newark group chose, instead, the *Gospel Trumpeter* as the name of their magazine. Both groups claim to be "the church of God." Both claim to be God's true reformation. Both call believers out of Babylon into the light of the truth.

Which of these five groups, including the Church of God (Anderson, Indiana) is the true heir of Brother D.S. Warner? Does it really matter? Brother Tasker was convinced that Brother Warner's original vision, that is, his vision of the New Testament church of God, was correct. This was while he was yet a part of the Churches of God (Winebrennarian). But Brother Warner went astray later on, so Brother Tasker believed, when he began to "find" his little band of holiness believers in obscure biblical texts believed to prophesy their coming into being as God's final reformation, through which God would complete what he had begun in the Protestant Reformation. The "front seat" again!

That view began to be questioned from within the ranks

very early on. Brother Warner's own wife, Sarah Keller, could not accept it. Undoubtedly others agreed with her. After Brother Warner's death and the move to Moundsville, West Virginia, disaffection and excommunication–for a variety of reasons, but certainly including this central claim–were not uncommon. And it is likely that quite a few left on their own accord, not because they did not believe in salvation in Christ, or holiness, or unity, but because they could not accept the rigidity, narrowness, exclusiveness, and intolerance to which the come-out doctrine seemed to lead.

### Comeoutism in Eclipse

By the 1940s, comeoutism and the notion that 1880 was prophesied in Scripture had come to be increasingly ignored by many, spoken against in public by others. The day of the "influential brethren" was rapidly waning and a new generation of leaders was on the scene, a generation not, on the whole, committed to these doctrines. They were, of course, still the "official" view of the Gospel Trumpet Company, which consistently refused either to publish or to print any other view. But the word was getting out, nonetheless.

Sometime in the early 1940s, Charles W. Naylor (who died in 1950) privately published his extended pamphlet, "The Teachings of D.S. Warner and His Associates." After a life-time of service, study, and reflection, he had concluded that Brother Warner was wrong in his "prophetic" interpretation of the scriptures, that "comeoutism" was wrong, and that the new vision of the Church of God was essentially correct. Here is one of his statements on comeoutism:

> Brother Warner expected all Christians to be brought into this movement in a single generation–this I know from his own lips. He said so publicly in a meeting I attended and from others I learn that he repeated the statement at other times and in other places. His expectations are not only far from realized, but they have not even begun to be

realized. No large number of Christians [has] heard and accepted our "come out" message. Of those who have come to us from other movements, by far the greater number have come not because of hearing that message but because they wanted the salvation we preach or because they sought greater freedom among a more spiritual people. . . . Our "come out" message has never proved effective except in a most limited way, and I see no reason to expect it to be more effective in the future. If we should count the number of those who were Christians in the denominations and who heard our prophetic message and because of it came to us, we would find the number surprisingly small, the percentage of our whole number very low. There are more Christians in the denominations every year in spite of our message. There are probably a million persons converted in the world every year. The hope of ever bringing these Christians into our group is futile.

Brother Naylor's view was not the view of a disgruntled fringe, but a studied view increasingly held both within the corridors of power and in the Church at large. In an introductory statement to his pamphlet, he says, "about thirty representative ministers have read this paper and it has been judged to be of sufficient importance to warrant a wider study, therefore a committee has been appointed to provide copies of it for others who may be interested in it."

On reading Brother Naylor, I can easily believe I'm reading Brother Tasker. It is highly likely that "Charlie Naylor," as Brother Tasker called him—and who was his good friend—had read *An Appeal* and other of Brother Tasker's many writings.[1] And his course may well have

---

[1] I've just recently learned that Brother Tasker owned and had carefully read Brother Naylor's book. David Davis of British Columbia (who was one of the young members of the congregation we attended with the Taskers) has just sent me a copy of it, liberally sprinkled with Brother Tasker's familiar handwriting. In the main, he agrees wholeheartedly with his

136

been altered by them. But perhaps both of them were responding to a slowly growing awareness in the Church that scriptural "prophecy" was, in fact, scriptural misreading. It was, so to speak, "in the air" they all breathed. Brother Naylor was longer in accepting it than were others, but eventually he came to embrace it as well.

In my Church of God heritage, I learned very little about D.S. Warner or comeoutism or scriptural "prophesy" of 1880 and the evening light. To be honest, I can't remember even hearing about any of it. In my late teens, I entered Alberta Bible Institute (now Gardner College), the very place one would expect such teaching. But it was 1949 and by then it was, perhaps, going "out of fashion." I later completed a B.A. degree at Pacific Bible College (now Warner Pacific College), founded by A.F. Gray and Otto F. Linn, both stalwarts of the Church. I can't recollect hearing much of anything about comeoutism there either.

What am I saying? Simply that by the late 1940s an alternative vision of the Church of God appears to have been quite firmly established, no matter what our "official" literature might say. But only in some places. It is quite possible that in the mid-western United States, as opposed to western Canada and the northwest United States, the old vision was still strong—otherwise Brother Naylor's pamphlet might at least have been *printed* by Warner Press' commercial printing division (as they did with Otto F. Lynn's volume dealing with the book of Revelation).

---

friend "Charlie" (they began together in Moundsville). Brother Naylor writes: "Denominations were always wrong; they are still wrong, but most of God's people are in them and he works among his people wherever they are" (p.17). To which Brother Tasker responds: "And we have only made another!" Then asks, "[But] may not a thing be 'wrong' and yet not be sin?" Brother Naylor later observes: "One can be a member of a denomination and yet be wholly unsectarian" (p.18). To which Brother Tasker responds: "Then why worry about getting rid of them? A village or city would not be improved by doing away with home units." He felt that a variety of groups was not harmful to the Gospel or to Christian unity. "Everything depends upon the spirit possess-ed," he said. After all, unity comes from "being fill with and characterized by the one Spirit of Christ."

## Diverse Visions

What we've been talking about is one vision replacing another. Must this inevitably be the case? Or can those holding differing visions of the same reality learn to live with each other? In order to do that, the visions themselves would of course have to have a built in tolerance of, even appreciation for, such diversity. Certainly that has never been the case with comeoutism. Nor could it be. The whole point is to present only one option, asserting it to be the only good option ("revealed" and all that goes with that belief). The alternative is simply too terrible to think about. Even to suggest a possible alternative was to court excommunication at one point.

But, as Brother Naylor insists, the option of comeoutism simply has not worked. Brother Tasker had already suggested that in 1921 when he said that if all he had had to go on was the *Gospel Trumpet* he would never have been drawn to the Church of God. Comeoutism was simply too unattractive (and, for him, too biblically and intellectually implausible).

I am not a part of the American cult of church growth, which seems to insist that numerical growth is the primary criterion by which the spiritual and theological fitness of a Church is to be judged. (Bigger is not necessarily better, in spite of the prevailing American cultural view to the contrary.) But neither would I want to argue that numerical growth indicates *nothing* about the vitality of a Church.

So it may be that Brother Naylor was right in asserting that if a doctrine is to be judged by its fruits, then the quite limited response to comeoutism questions its pragmatic truthfulness. The very slow growth of the Church of God in its first two generations—when similar Churches and movements were growing quite rapidly—certainly suggests that comeoutism could produce only very limited numerical results. (Nor was the *quality* always that great! In that, Sarah Keller Warner may have been right.)

In the beginning of the Church of God, toleration of alternative visions would not have been possible. We had not yet achieved sufficient critical mass. But with the changing of the times within the Church—and the society as a whole–and the increasing influx of those from other traditions (but not in response to the come-out message, so Brother Naylor insists), the original homogeneity of the fellowship began to be lost. The very diversity of traditions and stories changed the way we thought about ourselves and others. Toleration was now possible.

We are no longer as a whole given to our early exclusivisms. And our critical mass has greatly expanded. Now, as John W.V. Smith suggests, it is no longer possible to say confidently just what Church of God theology is. The proper word is probably "theologies." What we have is diverse visions under a much larger and more inclusive umbrella. Brother Tasker would have enjoyed the lively interplay, the intellectual stimulation, the freedom to agree and disagree without the itch to excommunicate those thought too "liberal" or "conservative" or "fundamentalist" (now there is a trio of nearly-useless labels!), and the great possibilities for cooperation and mutual learning for all of us. In short, for spiritual growth based on solid biblical principles focused on Christ alone.

### Movement or Church?

From all of this, a second question begins to emerge. Is the Church of God (Anderson, Indiana) today a "reformation movement" or is it a Church like other Churches? Was it ever really a reformation movement? If so, has it ceased to be so–and when did it cease to be so? These questions are very much with us today.

Most of us think we know what a "movement" is. But after these past months up to my chin in historical prose, I'm no longer so sure. Recently, I've been reading H.A. Drake's new book, *Constantine and the Bishops: the Politics of Intolerance.* In writing about Christianity, he has this to say:

> Organizationally, Christianity was a "movement," that is, an organization devoted to effecting change in the public sphere. Because there is something movements want to change, they are driven by a sense of purpose; they have an agenda. . . . Chris-

tianity was clearly a social movement, not a protest movement. Social movements . . . advance their goals by building their own alternative institutions, co-existing with the current political order rather than seeking to dismantle it.

Drake goes on to argue that "social" (and religious) movements "must find a way to maintain a separate identity, the special characteristics that set them apart from the dominant group . . . in which they developed and which give their members a way to distinguish themselves from non-members." However, he says, the movement must have enough in common with the dominant group to be able to attract new members (Drake 2000:76-77).

A "successful movement," Drake says, is heterogeneous (or consists of a variety of dissimilar elements and parts). That is, its adherents come from a variety of sources within the dominant society: from many walks of life; from many traditions; and from a variety of cultural worlds. "It is essential, therefore," he argues, "for the movement to identify and articulate clearly those central beliefs and goals and to impress its members that differences in any ways other than these are unimportant" (p.77).

Heterogeneity (as opposed to homogeneity), however, brings with it its own set of problems. As Drake points out, it creates the mass needed to stay alive and grow, but it lends itself to internal division. Therefore, he says, "to hold a heterogeneous movement together, leaders must be skilled in the use of tact and ambiguity." It must "count as 'in' those who have not explicitly opted out" (pp. 78-79).

### What We Were Historically

Given Drake's definition of a movement (and remember, it's not the only definition around of a movement—but we need some reasonable definition as a starting point  if we are to think with clarity) did the little band of come-outers centered in Grand Junction, Michigan by the mid-1880s qualify? They certainly defined themselves as a movement, a "reformation movement" in which a "restoration of pure, primitive Christianity" was occurring. It could even sing of the "mighty reformation sweeping o'er the land." This movement represented a "gathering back to primitive conditions," "back to Zion," "sanctified and cleansed from all sin and traditions," the only "present, visible reformation movement," into which all true believers everywhere are to be invited in this final period known as "the evening light" (see H.M. Riggle, "A Present Restoration Work," *Gospel Trumpet,* January 1 and 8, 1925).

This self-conscious sense of being a "movement" brought into existence by God to spread the word of "the evening light now shining" was the center of this group's self-identity. Its goal? To call out of "sect Babylon" all of those whose hearts were true before God, God's "true sheep" scattered throughout Christendom during the "cloudy day" of denominational confusion. All of these believers were to be one in spirit and doctrine through having been gathered by God into one sheepfold, the church of God, Zion on earth, the Heavenly Jerusalem.

Again the question, did this small handful of "saints in the evening light" constitute a movement? Or were they merely a sect on the fringe of things like half a hundred others bouncing around the outer walls of the ecclesiastical world during the same period? They had a sense of separate self-identity. They had some core doctrines–apart from those they shared with the Churches of the day. And they had enough in common with the church world of their day to attract new members. It sounds like they were a movement–or at least set to become one.

But, the social movement of which Drake speaks, seeks to "effect change in the public sphere." In this sense, the "saints in the evening light" were not a movement. Sect Babylon could not be changed; it was under the judgment of God–or so they proclaimed. From the beginning, they condemned Babylon as "the mother of harlots" and engaged in a set of rhetorical exercises known as "threshing Babylon" (which I understand as flailing in order to separate grain from weed seeds and thus garner the grain). The end result was an intentional and total separation from everyone and everything that was not "us."

The Holiness Movement–as a counter example for the sake of comparison–sought to awaken the churches to the biblical call to sanctification and holy living. "Coming out" was out of the world, not necessarily the Church to which one belonged. To be sure, the end result was a number of new churches, each one committed to a particular way of understanding the core doctrines of the Movement itself. But that may have been the law of unintended consequences as much as anything else. It was not what they started out to do. Their heterogeneity did, in this case, lead to internal division and fragmentation. Apparently, the leaders were neither sufficiently tactful nor ambiguous.

In the case of the Evening Light saints, tact and ambiguity were neither welcomed nor observed. The leadership, particularly after the death of Brother Warner, made it quite clear what one must believe and do in order to belong. If anyone dared to disagree or do otherwise, they became history in short order. Homogeneity was the order of the day. Heterogeneity was heterodoxy (or heresy, if you prefer) in disguise. All must think, believe, confess, and act alike. This was not always the way things turned out, but it's what was demanded.

As far as we know, whatever heterogeneity and heterodoxy existed among the saints was well-contained until after the move to Moundsville, West Virginia in 1898. Now the prophet was gone and the manager was in control; critical mass was increasing; and doctrinal division began to manifest itself among the ministers. In the next two decades, excommunications and defections were much more common than some of us would like to think.

That, in itself, doesn't sound very movement-like. A "successful" movement, Drake says, is one that is able to count as being "in" those who have not counted themselves "out." Counting adherents out who had counted themselves in seems the wrong way around. And yet it happened. In Brother Tasker's view, this characterized a sect, not a movement. And not just a sect, but a very sectarian sect.

But we are not yet done with Drake. In his view of

things, a social movement (such as religious groups often are) was not the only kind of movement possible. Some movements, he said, are best described as "protest movements." Such movements are characterized by againstness: they are against another system or, as is often the case, *any* other system. They are concerned with revolutionary change and "seek to win by direct frontal assault" on the system or systems which they oppose (p. 76). Given this definition, the early Church of God does sound like a protest movement.

The "comeouters" were not interested in reforming the denominational system of their world. Like protest movements in general, their goal was to tear down, dismantle, or displace the old system with a new system of their own making. If that could not be done, at least they could provide an alternative system into which all of God's true sheep could be gathered. Babylon had the smell of death about it. It was beyond reformation. Only those who came "out of her" into the pure evening light could be saved in the end—and that end was thought to be in their lifetime.[1]

---

[1] By the mid-1920s, at least, a few of the "influential brethren" may well have been rethinking this earlier position . I referred above to H.M. Riggle's two articles, "A Present Restoration Work" (*Gospel Trumpet*, January 1 and 8, 1925) (published, interestingly, just prior to the Editor's condemnation of Brothers Tasker and Bruffett later that month). These articles seem to take a "softer" approach to Christians who have not "come out" of Babylon. Some people need more time to grasp "the truth." We must "be patient and show all Christian courtesy and love," rather than manifesting a "better-than-thou" spirit. "There are thousands of precious saints who are just as good as we are, but they have never seen the clear light on the unity of God's people," Brother Riggle says. "Because of lack of teaching they have not been able to discern clearly the body of Christ, the church. It is our mission and work to give them the light." One can, I think, infer from these articles that if one of these "precious saints" heard this "truth" and rejected it, it would be tantamount to rejecting the whole gospel. If, however, some of this great multitude of "precious saints" never heard it, they would remain "precious saints," but die unenlightened by this ultimate and final truth—saved, but "so as by fire." Is this position at some point between that of Brothers Smith and Tasker? It seems so to me.

Beginning in Moundsville–and probably earlier–a few individuals, at least, began to voice different views. They were generally in agreement with the majority view that God's true sheep are scattered throughout the churches, but quite disagreed with the way the "so what?" question was answered. Should they come out? Or should they remain within the system as salt and leaven and light, witnesses to the great reformation work of God in the life of the Churches–who, for the most part, were not going to listen to a radical bunch of flailers from the hills and hollows on the other side of the river in any event?

Brother Tasker spoke for a committed minority–those who had not counted themselves "out"–when he argued that God's work of reformation encompassed Christendom itself. No Church was, or could be, that reformation, since that reformation was God's work being done through true believers everywhere, that is, the church of God spoken of in scripture. The Church of God, however, could be a movement–like others in existence--to further that work of reformation. Could, that is, if it would cleanse itself of the narrow, sectarian spirit that so distressingly gripped it.

### What We Are Today

Eventually, this "social movement" view won out in the struggle for dominance. As we have noted, by the 1950s, we could speak with a widely-echoed voice of our concern for "a united church for a divided world" which could be achieved only through cooperative effort with all concerned Christians everywhere. The Christian Brotherhood Hour thus reflected this triumph of a long suppressed or ignored minority vision (and to be ignored is often far worse than being suppressed).

If we have been a movement in the past, are we any longer a movement? Does it matter? Some say we have lost our way as a movement and, yes, that matters. The solution? Go back to the point at which we began to lose it and begin again. Thus, a restoration movement.

But a moment's conversation reveals that the movement they have in mind is really Drake's protest movement, a faithful remnant preaching a renewed come-out doctrine and practicing separation from those who hold contrary views on everything from scripture to states rights. They do not seek to add to the richness of diversity now to be found among us and thus further the dialogue that leads to truth and truthfulness, but to dislodge what they find offensive, replacing it with their own view of things–an essentially primitivist view.

Do such restoration movements have a prophetic function in the wider body in which they arise? Indeed, they may have. They often–but not inevitably and in every case–see things that need to be corrected, directions that need to be changed, oversights that need to be brought to public view, questions that need to be addressed, or priorities that need to be rethought. Without such prophetic groups, groups that do not count themselves "out," (nor count as "out" those with whom they disagree) all of us are the poorer. (At the same time, such groups need the larger community in which they arise. Without restraint and accountability, they tend to spin out of orbit and become separatist and exclusive.)

As we should quite easily be able to see in the events of our own history, movements built around prophets soon become something else in the hands of their successors, whose primary concern seems inevitably to be to con-solidate, conserve, and control the movement. When prophets give way to administrators, the end of a movement is usually in sight. (Recall what happened in India!) It begins to take on structure and organization and to accumulate all of the rest of the institutional trappings common to churches. It might not out-Rome Rome itself, as Brother Tasker thought might be beginning to happen in the Church of God in the 1920s, but it certainly can no longer "outmove" the prophet who served as its midwife.

Perhaps all of this is simply my roundabout way of saying that the Church of God now is a Church—whatever it may have been in the past. The term "movement" does not apply to it. It looks like a Church, feels like a Church, and acts like a Church. It is structured like a Church existing in American culture, with all of its "gospel-like" commitments to corporate America and its hierarchical models of organization. (Talk about Catholic attempts to baptize pagan gods! That ought to bring out the prophets among us! I don't see many lining up, however.)

I have a lot of problems with that. But, like my mentor, I have even more problems with those who insist on drawing exclusive boundaries—supposedly on God's behalf—to shut out people like us who think Christians can exist in diverse "families" without needing to occupy the same ecclesiastical space. They seem to believe that holiness and unity can be found only in one human organization which we have chosen to call Church—or "movement." In truth, we have often mistaken allegiance to a set of doctrines and practices for allegiance to Christ. That they are never one and the same thing has been lost on us at various times in our collective past.

Unity is rather to be found in our devotion to Christ, not in uniform acceptance of a set of unchanging doctrines and practices (and, as Brother Tasker insisted, no set of doctrines or practices is inspired anyway; nor is any interpretation of scripture). The crucified Christ, Brother Tasker believed, is our gathering place. As Gordon A. Schieck, longtime Church of God missionary to India, used to say, "Come to the cross and we'll meet you there."

That great multitude gathered around the crucified Christ is the church of God. But our allegiance is not to any particular institutional expression of that church, such as the Church of God. It is to Christ and then to all who are in him. Our primary concern, Brother Tasker believed, was to build up the church of God. If, at the same time, it builds up the Church of God, well and good. If it builds up other Churches, perfecting them into the image of Christ, that is good also. Our problem, he said, was that we had gotten the cart before the horse. When that happened, we ceased being a true reformation movement. I think I agree. Probably. If we ever were!

In the 1950s, the Christian Brotherhood Hour (today some of us, at least, would insist on finding a more inclusive title) may have been our best public expression of what it means to be a movement. It was, as we noted earlier, an attempt "to call all Christians everywhere" to work together for a united church in a divided ecclesiastical world. Far from being a come-out call, this was a call for mutual love, acceptance, and action.

Perhaps the Christian Brotherhood Hour was based on a genuine perception of the Church of God as a movement (which, I think, is how Brother Tasker perceived the Church of God in India from the beginning, up until the arrival of Floyd W. Heinly and the Missionary Manual). In every broadcast, CBH reiterated its call to "all Christians everywhere to work together for a united church for a divided world." Idealistic, perhaps. But arguably biblical.

We find no notion here that the Church of God is the church of God into which all who are baptized into Christ enter, or that those so baptized must come out of sectism into "this visible reformation," as Brother Riggle has it. The CBH was thus a voice of the Church of God calling Christians to unite in spirit and in Christ's mission. This is certainly not the *organic* unity being called for by Brother Riggle, for example, for whom the church of God was visible and visibly united. It is, rather, a *spiritual* unity based upon a common allegiance to Christ.

How widely shared this vision was is another question. Was it simply the ideal vision of those who happened to be in power at that time? Was the Church of God largely somewhere else on this matter? Were the new "influential brethren" in Anderson making the mistake to which we've long been prone, namely, in assuming that the whistle drives the train?

Given our regionalisms and our diversity, it is difficult to say how widely shared this ideal was. Some of us know from our own regional experience of the Church that some yet today do not share it. That a good many more did not nearly fifty years ago is quite likely. But at least some segments of the Church back then shared that vision—and it is likely that segments of other Churches who listened to the program regularly did as well.

My sense is that it is probably shared by a majority today—at least among those who have bothered to think about and discuss the issue. So, at least at times we have sounded like a movement. Whether this has been true to any great extent at the grassroots may be debated. (Since our histories tend to be written from the top down and by persons who are not at the grassroots, we really haven't any good way of answering this question.)

## The Temptations of Power

One final concern. Everything that would count for evidence among historians indicates that it is probable that Brother Tasker was the victim of an abuse of ecclesiastical power. He had ruffled too many feathers in high places and he was, it seems, something of an intellectual threat to some of the "influential brethren." For this reason, apparently, his letter of apology to the Missionary Board, expressing his decision to comply with The Missionary Manual and cooperate with the Missionary Board's Field Secretary for India, was withheld from the full Board.

Who did this really does not matter. Since the President of the Board later admitted publicly that the letter had been received in the Board office, it is likely that he had seen it himself upon its reception. But we can't be sure. The Executive Secretary-Treasurer may have made a unilateral decision not to reveal the letter to the Board. I think it more likely, however, that it was an "unofficial" Executive Committee decision—one of those conversations not to be overheard or recorded in any official Minutes. They happen now and they happened then.

### The Why Question

My question is, rather, *why* the letter was withheld. Was Brother Tasker perceived as such a threat to the Missionary Board budget that he could no longer be tolerated? The Board was having major and ongoing financial problems. Many local pastors were not overly enthused about sending overseas local dollars they saw as being so badly needed at home in the first place. For most of them, overseas missions were certainly not a priority. In addition, the Church was characterized by a very nervous ethos. Gospel Trumpet literature over the years had itself seen to that. Critically outspoken missionaries could quite easily cause a fuss and pastors responded by withholding money. The Board was truly between a rock and a hard place.

Did some of the "influential brethren" see this as an opportunity to rid themselves of an intellectually brilliant and outspoken critic? I think it not unfair or demeaning to say that Brother Tasker had no intellectual equals among the Anderson brethren and their supporters. His intellectual force was such that those with some such inclinations responded positively to his arguments–or particularly to his style of argumentation. Those who considered it their God-given role to function as the teaching authority of the Church (at least "Roming" with Rome?), which is what the Editor's Chair represented, were not infrequently being challenged by him.

I've mentioned in passing Brother Tasker's challenge to Brother Smith's *Revelation Explained.* He believed it to represent poor interpretive practice. To base so much theological certitude on figurative and symbolic language, particularly when those interpretive conclusions so frequently contradicted the Gospels and Paul, was poor scholarship, so he thought. He later told me that Brother Smith refused to discuss the book with him and would not respond to his letter. Did he ignore Brother Tasker because he feared Brother Tasker's ability to summon both reason and scholarly opinion to his aid? Or was it simply a case of "What I have written, I have written?"

Again, I don't really know. But if that letter was deliberately withheld–and everything seems to point in that direction–then it was withheld for what the "brethren" felt were very good reasons. To plot Brother Tasker's demise simply because of his brusque and uncooperative responses to their attempts to get the missionaries and Indian leaders "in line" by sending out a largely unqualified and inexperienced young man as the India field director was not sufficient cause—and particularly when the withheld letter had assured them that he would cooperate fully in spite of his deep misgivings. That would likely have been the end of the matter right then and there.

Therefore, as much as I am saddened by the idea, I can only conclude–while wearing my historian's hat at least—that two or three of the brethren had decided Brother Tasker was a threat both to the work and to them personally. He had to be gotten rid of. They would not likely have a better opportunity. I think they were sincere in saying they felt very badly about having to do it. But, as unfortunate as it was, it was for the good of "the cause." "It is better for one man to die . . . ," so to speak. They had the power to do it and so they did it.

## The Abuse of Power

If most of this be the case, then we are left with a probable abuse of power by those who professed, at any rate, to be "servants" of the Church. However reluctantly they may have used their power to silence and remove a troublesome critic, the fact remains, they did so and in doing so may have violated a sacred trust. Even if we could explain fully why it was done, that would not by any measure justify doing it. Such an action is not only unethical, but also immoral–and may fall into the category of "misconduct of public office."

But that's the problem with this social "good" we call power. The temptation to use it for personal advantage and gain–or to misuse it in a seemingly good cause–is often stronger than the people in whom it's vested. Power does not corrupt (and Lord Acton did not say that, in spite of all those who quote him as having done so), but it certainly does *tend* to do so (which Lord Acton did say). Most unfortunately, even those within the Church who profess to be "servant leaders" (surely an oxymoron in a rigidly hierarchically structured system!) are not always immune to this tendency.

We would like to think otherwise, of course. Given our tendency to think the best about everyone and to say only what is "nice," we hate to think of those in leadership being involved in such unethical behavior. In fact, we tend to write it out of our histories, covering it over with "spiritual" language. Some of this writing gives the impression that these people were paragons of virtue and spirituality, incapable of anything so common or mean. When such writing is "debunked," it makes most of us feel uncomfortable and even betrayed.

But we must keep in mind that the temptation to use the power of position against those with whom we disagree and who we see as a threat to all we stand for is very great indeed. Those who serve the Church have, under our "governmental" system, almost quite literally to place themselves in the hands of one or more Boards, committees, or associations. When they persist in doing that with which we disagree doctrinally or philosophically, the temptation to use the power available to us to silence them or remove them altogether can be very strong. "They can go somewhere else if they don't like our rules"–as Brother Tasker was told, when he protested that the Indian leaders of the Church were opposed to the Missionary Board's policies for India.

And they would be, in a limited sense, right to say so *if the organization with which they had voluntarily affiliated had been openly and avowedly hierarchical in structure.* But it was, in fact, quite the opposite. It identified itself as a community of saints under the rule of the Holy Spirit. It stood dead against archbishops, bishops, superintendents, councils, and synods. Brother Tasker and the Indian leaders, therefore, expected collegial discussion and dialogue, with each learning from the other. It was inevitable that they would see "man-rule" under the circumstances–and very top-down and authoritarian man-rule at that. As far as they were concerned, it was a denial of what it means to be "the church of God."

Even more serious than the misuse of power, however, is the use of position and power to *assure position and power.* By small and subtle incremental changes in the "rules," governing structures can eventually become self-perpetuating. Those with the power can thus see to it that they stay powerful and in control.

And, make no mistake about it, it's the powerful who make the rules. To be sure, they are usually clever enough to convince the majority that it was really the idea of the majority all along (generally by involving the majority in structured and extended discussion exercises). That's what good leadership is all about, isn't it? Great system–if you control it. The powerful may not at all be cynical, but sincerely believe it is for everyone's good, or for the good of the cause, that they remain in power. After all, who is better qualified or has greater right? (Meritocracy is, surely, one of our basic North American cultural values. Perhaps this is the gentle side of social Darwinism.)

Knowing full well what was going on, Brother Tasker had little option but to find another association if he were to fulfill his missionary calling. Those who had power over him had decided he was too great a risk to their vision of things. They were, of course, passionately convinced that they were right and that God had chosen them to preserve and promote "this reformation." They were "servant leaders" (meaning, of course, God's servants through whom he ruled "theocratically.") Authority had been given them by the election and anointing of God and they were "bound by conscience" (Brother Smith's words) to exercise that authority. If anyone believed otherwise, they must be removed for the good of "the reformation."

## Conclusion

It's time to end this rather morose reflection–and this story. These are the questions and concerns that seemed to keep surfacing, no matter how many times I pushed them back under. They are not questions I had before I ever began to write (at least, not that I am aware of), but emerged slowly and persistently. This is, quite simply, where the story has led me. These are questions I must, then, ask of our collective past if I'm to understand more fully who and what I am. Among other things, I am *homo historicus*, a historical being. Without its beginning, my story is incomplete and the meaning of it greatly altered. (I would then be, as some literary figure whose name I've long since forgotten once wrote: "a leaf unaware that it is attached to a tree.")

The same is true of *our* story as the Church of God. Brother Tasker's story is so much a part of it that to fail to tell it–in at least all of the dimensions on which we've touched–is to violate our own story. It is to opt for *heritage* rather than *history*. History does not, always and necessarily, lead us to happy and uplifting endings–as it surely has not in this case. Often the endings are sad, unsettling, filled with pathos and regret. But *c'est la vie!* That's life as it comes to us, unbidden and often unwanted.

152

# WORKS AND MATERIALS CITED

Allen, Roland. *Missionary Methods, St. Paul's Or Ours?* New
York: Revell, 1912.

Anderson, Beverly C. *A History of the Church of God in Ontario
1882-1955.* M.Div. Thesis. Anderson: Archives.

Brown, Charles E. *When the Trumpet Sounded.* Anderson:
Warner Press, 1951.

Byrum, Noah H. "Our Anderson Home." Anderson University:
Church of God Archives.

Byrum, Russell R. Interview, 1978. Notes in the possession of
the author, Anderson, Indiana.

Caldwell, Mack M. Interview, 1979. Notes in the possession of
the author, Anderson, Indiana.

Crose, John D. Interview, 1979. Notes in the possession of the
author, Anderson, Indiana.

Crose, Lester A. *Passport for a Reformation.* Anderson: Warner
Press, 1981.

Drake, H.A. *Constantine and the Bishops: the Politics of Intolerance.* Baltimore: Johns Hopkins University Press, 2000.

Geertz, Clifford. *Available Light: Anthropological Reflections on
Philosophical Topics.* Princeton University Press, 2000.

Khan, Aurelius D. Personal letter to D. Welch, November 21,
1979. In author's possession.

-----------------------. Interview, Calcutta, India 1980. Notes in
author's possession.

Khan, John A.D. *India⫰s Millions.* Moundsville: Gospel Trumpet
Company, 1903.

Loewen, James W. *Lies Across America: What Our Historic
Sites Got Wrong.* New York: the New Press, 1999.

Missionary Board Correspondence, 1916-1936. Anderson
University: Church of God Archives.

Missionary Board Minutes, 1909-1936. Anderson University:
Church of God Archives.

Mondol, S.K. Letter of Recommendation of George P. Tasker,
1946. Anderson University: Church of God Archives.

Morrison, John A. *As the River Flows.* Anderson: Anderson
College Press, 1962.

Naylor, Charles W. *The Teachings of D.S. Warner and His Associates.* Published privately in the early 1940s.

Phillips, Harold L. *The Miracle of Survival.* Anderson: Warner Press, 1979.

Reardon, E.A. "The Problem of Christian Unity." In *Following the Light,* Edited by Barry L. Callen. Warner Press, 2000.

------------------. *Our Ministerial Letter: A Message to Young Ministers.* Vol. II, No. 10. Gospel Trumpet Co., 1915.

Smith, Frederick G. *Revelation Explained.* Anderson: Gospel Trumpet Company, 1909.

------------------. *The Last Reformation.* Anderson: Gospel Trumpet Company, 1919.

------------------. "Editorial." *Gospel Trumpet,* May 15, 1924.

------------------. "Another Church Crisis at Hand." *Gospel Trumpet,* January 22, 1925.

------------------. *A Brief Sketch of the Origin, Growth, and Distinctive Doctrine of the Church of God Movement.* Anderson: Gospel Trumpet Company, 1927.

------------------. Personal Papers. Anderson University: Archives.

Tasker, George P. "How I Became a Foreign Missionary." *Gospel Trumpet,* November 17, 1921.

------------------. "Intense Interest of Our Calcutta Student Work." *Gospel Trumpet,* March 23, 1923.

------------------. *An Appeal to the Free and Autonomous Churches of Christ in the Fellowship of the Evening Light.* Calcutta, India, 1924.

------------------. Personal Letter to E.A. Reardon, June 21, 1935. In author's possession, Anderson IN.

------------------. Personal Letter to the Criswell Family, November 10, 1940. Anderson University: Archives.

------------------. Personal Letter to Rev. T.R. Phillips, 1943. Anderson University: Archives.

------------------. Personal Papers. Anderson University: Church of God Archives.

Tasker, Mona Moors. Personal letters to D. Welch. In author's possession, Anderson IN.

# INDEX